POSITIVE THINKING

How To Stop Focusing On Nonsense And
Live A Better Life

By Vishal Pandey

TABLE OF CONTENTS

INTRODUCTION

"It will not work. Don't try."

"Success is for talented people, not me."

"I am not good enough."

"How could I be so stupid?"

"I will mess it up again."

"I can't do anything right."

Thoughts like these stand between you and all the things you want and truly deserve. These inner thoughts have been in your mind for so long that you consider them a normal part of the day.

I call these thoughts our *inner critic*.

Your inner critic re-affirms lies about yourself that you have internalized to be true. It becomes especially loud and vicious when you make a mistake. That is its dirty little trick to corner you down. It overwhelms you.

This book is dedicated to people experiencing these self-defeating inner dialogs. It aims to revitalize your mind to stop repressing your true potential, take charge, and start living with more conviction.

I believe life is 10% what happens to you and 90% how you react to it. This book is all about that 90% part. Sometimes, it is better to react with "no reaction". Because when you react emotionally to something or someone, you give your power away.

Your thoughts matter (a lot actually!)

I was quite young when I read "as a man thinketh, so is he." I remember shaking my head, thinking about how it could be so wrong. My parents always told me that thinking is for lazy people.

I failed to realize the amount of truth in that quote.

It would be much later, after years of reading books and analyzing neuroscience researches, I got my mind around how true that quote had been. We have learned more about the human brain in the last two decades than the entire previous human history.

Have you paid attention to how much your actions & behavior is determined by your thoughts? You can see its influence in each step you take, move you make, and the words you say.

"Happiness is when what you think, what you say, and what you do are in harmony." - **Mahatma Gandhi**

A negative mind will never give you a positive life. You have to let go of certain thoughts to become a person that you were meant to be. The good news is... in the middle of every difficulty lies an opportunity. You do have the ability to change your thoughts. With some dedication and effort, change is definitely possible.

But before we start, let's talk about expectations. Your negative thought habit was formed over the span of years and it cannot change in a day or two. Please do not expect instant results. But I assure you, changes are definitely possible if you persist with the advice and exercises coming up.

There are clear, actionable steps laid out in the book which had helped me and several others overcome depression and negative thinking habit. But you have to promise me to do the exercises and use what you learn as you go through the day.

I wish you all the joy, passion, confidence, and love that you want and rightfully deserve.

Let's begin, shall we?

CHAPTER 1
HOW TO NOT TAKE THINGS PERSONALLY?

There is only one way to avoid criticism: do nothing, say nothing, and be nothing. If you do anything, people will have something to say about it. With the freedom of speech comes the freedom to criticize. It's amazing that everyone has an opinion on how you should live your life.

But criticism is an important part of life. It shows you are doing something. Criticism is the price you pay for having ambition. If you are never criticized, you may not be doing much that makes a difference. Learning to not take criticism personally is something we all can benefit from. Take criticism seriously, but never personally. If there is truth in the criticism, learn from it. Otherwise, just let it go. In this chapter, we will look at exactly how to do that.

It's not about you

Here's the truth - 99% of the time how people behave is not about you. It's about them. How they are behaving depends on a long list of underlying reasons. And even if you are on that list, you probably rank at the very bottom. There are several reasons which determine other people's behavior and most of the time they are not related to you at all. When someone disrespects you, be wary of the impulse to win their approval. Their disrespect is not a valuation of your worth. It is a signal of their character.

I cannot stress enough how important this is for your social interactions. If you do not internalize that people's behavior has nothing to do with you, you can never be truly free as far as your social life is concerned. Often people don't realize the price you paid to get to where you are today. They don't. And if you let each and every little comment shake you up, it's not healthy for your emotional health & self-confidence.

Let's look at an example. If a cashier in your bank acts rudely, you feel bad. That's pretty normal. You are a human being and it is perfectly all right to feel bad if somebody misbehaves with you. BUT when you go home RAGING and think about that incident for hours... THAT is not normal.

This is a cue that you need to learn about not taking things personally.

People have many underlying issues and agendas

By going with the cashier example above, you repeat that incident in your head again & again, each time, feeling increasingly worse. Along with your hatred towards that person, you might start to think about the REASONS for which he behaved in that way.

Now comes the really important part... Because you do not have any more information about him, you put the entire blame on yourself. And these thoughts have a vicious cycle. Thoughts, generally, start from "maybe I said something bad" to "I always say something bad" to "I am not a good person" to "I deserved it!"

These thoughts are really harmful to you. They hurt you on various levels – Your self-confidence, your self-worth, your emotional health, your physical health & your happiness.

Stop letting people who do so little for you, control so much of your mind, feelings, and emotions. Remind yourself time and time again that other people have many underlying problems that are not apparent on the surface. If you could see what they are going through in their life, your hatred would turn into sympathy.

Maybe that cashier is having chronic back pain which is making him irritating & rude, or maybe he had a divorce yesterday afternoon and his family life is in ruins. There could be a million reasons for his behavior which are not related to you at all.

Nothing others do is because of you. What they say or do is a reflection of their own reality, their own life. It says nothing about you but a LOT about them.

How can you be certain of what is going on in other people's head at any point in time? People will love you. People will hate you. And most of the time, it will have nothing to do with you.

They really don't know you personally, so you don't take what they say personally.

Different realities

Objective reality is an illusion. People live in their own little world and only see what they want to see. You will be shocked to find the number of times people are focused on themselves. You might think people are looking at you, judging you but in reality, people are caught up in their own little bubble. Everybody is looking at the world from a different set of eyes.

A quote I love related to this topic (forgot who said it) – "when you are in your twenties, you think that everyone is thinking about you. When you are in your forties, you think that nobody is thinking about you. And when you reach your sixties, you realize that nobody was thinking about you at all."

It's a bummer that this kind of realization comes at a very late point in life. But that's where good self-help books & autobiographies can be so helpful. A person, who went through various hardships all his life, decides to put down all that knowledge in an easy to read book... That's called a real opportunity. You can learn what he learned and use it whenever you face a similar situation.

Reality is different for each one of us. And the biggest problem for all of us is the image in our heads of how life should be. Some people view the world as a nice place with endless opportunities. Others view it as a horrible place where everybody else is out to get them. What we see with our eyes does not get straight into our minds untouched. It gets through many 'filters' first.

What we see gets filtered through our beliefs, our worldviews, memories of our past experiences, our attitude, our physical state, and even our current mood. These filters COLOR what we see and hear.

Let's say, somebody plucks a flower from a tree, what would you think? Would you get angry thinking what will happen if all people start doing that? Soon, there will be no flowers left in that tree. OR would you feel happy thinking that people do take time to admire little things in life, even in this fast-moving world...?

Notice the difference?

The meaning of an event is whatever you ascribe it to be. Objective reality only exists in our minds and nowhere else.

Don't let other people's opinion of you become your reality. They have a different view of the world, its people, and how things are. Don't blame yourself. It's not about you. You can try everything in your power to change their perception, and you will fail.

It took years of life experience to get an individual's perception up to this point. You cannot change it in an instant. Don't even try. Instead, realize the truth that the final proof of greatness is being able to endure criticism without resentment. Let it roll right off you.

Good or bad, depends on you

No one is good or bad. It all depends on the situation and each person's perspective towards him or her. Whatever you believe will seem to be true. You cannot control other people & their outlook. You can only control yourself. I suggest you deliberately try to find the good in everything.

Why?

Because life is just too short to live in misery and blame everything. Life goes faster than you think. Ask anyone in his fifties or sixties about how fast they felt decades went by. The answer is always the same – "pretty fast!" So love, laugh and try new things. Time will pass away. You can either spend it creating the life you want or spend it living the life you don't want. The choice is yours.

Never blame, complain, and take things personally. It's a fool's errand. Instead, focus on the more important things in your life, things which you are grateful for. Enjoy the little things in life because one day you will look back and realize they were the big things.

If somebody makes a sly comment on you or behaves rudely, brush it off. It's not about you. Think BIG and don't listen to people who tell you that it cannot be done. Life is too short to think small. When someone tells you it can't be done, it's more a reflection of their limitation, not yours.

It is always better to forget and move on. Not everyone will understand your journey. That's ok. You are here to live your life, not to make everyone understand. No use trying.

How to deal with a persistent problem?

Sometimes, you will find yourself in a situation where it is not possible to just forget and move on. What if one of your coworkers is rude OR you have a family member who is always making negative comments. You will have contact with these people on a daily basis.

How to handle such a situation?

First, in the light of the above information, ask yourself – what else could this (behavior) mean?

This question will shift your focus to other possible meanings for an apparent bad behavior. You will start to see reasons for their behavior which have nothing to do with you.

Second, if the person is constantly demeaning you, SPEAK UP. Let them know how you feel. A lot of times, people have no idea about how they are making you feel. Be clear. If there is a problem between you two, discuss and resolve it. Almost always, they will change their behavior around you.

If they don't, as the last straw, either minimize your interactions with that person or cut them out of your life completely. We already have enough problems. We certainly don't need more. Move to a new place. Shift to a different department. Get a new job. Do whatever you need to separate yourself from a situation like this.

As a side note, I would also suggest you work on building your self-esteem. Negativity does not affect a high self-esteem person emotionally. People with high self-esteem know their own values and don't identify themselves with other people's comments. They have control over their emotions and know how to deal with people effectively.

So that's it.

Knowledge has no value unless you USE it. Try to implement this information in your life. Even if it takes time, do it. It's worth it. Your happiness is worth it. Life is to be enjoyed, not endured. When you try to control everything, you enjoy nothing. Sometimes, you just need to relax, let go, and live in the moment.

Think less and live more.

CHAPTER 2
FEAR IS A LIAR

Fear kills more dreams than failure ever will. It stops people from believing in themselves, dreaming big, and live a fulfilling life. Too many of us are not living our dreams because we are living our fears.

Each one of us is afraid. We all are scared. But everything you possibly want is on the other side of fear. There is no other way. If you don't take control of your fear, then it will control you.

You need to have the upper hand. The fears we don't face become our limits. It will always block you from moving ahead in life. Whenever you take a step forward, it will always be there to stop you. And it becomes stronger as you get closer to your goal.

I was surprised to know that even great public speakers feel anxious before giving their speech. Just like everyone, they too are afraid of going on stage. But they don't let the fear stop them... and maybe that's what makes them "great".

Olivia Fox Cabane, author of the excellent book *'the charisma myth'*, reveals that she still deals with anxiety every time she goes on stage, even after 15 years of public speaking experience.

The fear will always be there. You only learn to deal with it. Don't let your fear of what could happen to make nothing happen.

As you gain experience, you will realize that fear is a liar. It's all smoke and mirrors. In real life, the fear of facing your fear is harder to overcome than the fear itself.

It's NEVER as bad as you think it will be.

Some people say F.E.A.R is 'false evidence appearing real'. That's a nice acronym. It represents fear for what it actually is - prediction of a possible bad outcome.

We are so afraid that there is a possibility of experiencing a bad outcome, we never even attempt to do something, even if there are more chances of succeeding than failing.

(Note: by the way, there is no such thing as failure. We will cover this in much more detail in an upcoming chapter.)

I believe F.E.A.R has two more meanings - "Forget Everything And Run" OR "Face Everything And Rise". The choice is always in your hands.

But not all fears are bad. It's good to pay attention to your fears and get to know what they represent. Some are actually good for you. Fear of heights keeps you safe by not allowing you to do anything dangerous on heights. Fear of snakes and other dangerous animals is good for your wellbeing. Fear of fire, electricity, and poisonous things are there to keep you safe.

Such kinds of fear are completely natural and even necessary. They keep you away from physical harm. They are important.

We need to push past fears which serve no purpose in today's modern society. Let's take the fear of public speaking for example. Researchers have conducted a survey on what's the scariest experience for people.

It turned out that people are more afraid of public speaking than death. What a shocker! Especially considering there's no actual physical harm involved in standing on stage and expressing your ideas.

Fear doesn't exist anywhere except in the mind. We tend to run negative mental movies in our minds that shut us down. Have you seen someone shaking when they stand on the stage? Is it a life-threatening situation? A tiger is coming to attack them on stage?

No.

Examine your fears. Find out which ones are good & which ones serve no purpose. Some fears like public speaking, being rejected, being disliked are stopping you from making things right.

Being aware of your fears is a great start, and overcoming them is the sign of a successful person. People who fail to go past their fears get stuck in the same situation for many years. Ask any achiever: what was the most important thing they did to reach the next level?

Almost always the answer would be - "overcoming my fear"

And 99.99% of the time, the sensation of anxiety is worse than the actual bad outcome. We can deal with a difficult situation when we experience it. It's the fear of these difficulties that do more harm than the actual experience itself.

We imagine the situation to be 100 times worse than it actually is and play this mental movie in our minds repeatedly. It intensifies feelings of fear in several folds. And finally, when we confront the actual situation, our mind reacts the way we trained it till now - It feels terrifying!

Let me share an example. In my childhood, I was a shy little kid. To increase my social confidence, my class teacher told me to read out a three-page essay in front of the whole class. I had three days to prepare.

Those three days felt like three centuries. I was so afraid of standing in front of people and their eyes looking at me, that I couldn't write one page of the essay.

I imagined all sorts of things- The whole class laughing at me, gossiping forever about how badly I did, no one talking to me, no friends, being alone forever... AND being laughed at for being alone.

It was the worst feeling ever!

On the third day, I silently went to the teacher's room and told her I am scared and couldn't write the essay because of it. My teacher understood it was my fear that needed to be dealt with.

She asked me to read only the half-page that I wrote and go back to my seat. I was still terrified but had to do it.

And I did it.

It was not half as bad as I imagined. Nobody laughed, nobody shouted at me, and nobody gossiped about me afterward. My friends were still willing to talk to me.

The whole incident gave me confidence, but more importantly, it taught me a lesson that the thing you fear most has no power. Your fear of it gives it power.

The only thing we have to fear is the fear itself.

This is something I want you to realize as well. There is no greater illusion than fear. The closer you move towards it, the smaller it would become. Facing the truth really will set you free.

Our human brain is highly sensitive to the possibility of pain. Even if the chances of success & failure are equal - 50:50, we tend to focus more on negative 50%. In worse cases (people with a negative attitude, depression, etc) mind tend to focus on negative even if the chances of a positive outcome are much higher, say 80:20.

Fear does not stop death, it stops life. To be happy, we must train our minds to focus on the positive. Because, by default, the mind will focus on pain more than pleasure, negative more than positive.

But why do we tend to focus more on the negative?

There are a lot of elements involved in forming this 'negative-focus': bad childhood experiences, family atmosphere, upbringing, the attitude of surrounding people, friends, peers, influences like TV, news, etc - all play a part in training your mind to focus primarily on the negative.

And that's not all. There is a biological reason behind the tendency of the mind to focus more on the negative. In the caveman times, when the human brain was still developing, the survival was very difficult. The choices we made were the difference between life and death.

It was more important to anticipate and avoid danger than gaining feelings of pleasure. Avoiding confrontation with a sabertooth tiger was preferred over finding food that may be found in the area.

In those harsh conditions, the human mind developed a tendency to focus more on negative than positive. Since then, the world changed around us. Conditions are much more favorable now, but we still have that same "safety" mechanism inside. We still focus more on negatives to avoid any 'possible' bad outcomes.

So, become comfortable with being afraid. Fear will ALWAYS be there, at every corner of life. There is no running away from it. You are designed by nature to experience fear.

But the interesting thing is, the majority of your fears (public speaking, social anxiety, being embarrassed, rejection, etc) are invalid today. They serve no purpose. If you want to change yourself, you have to push past your fears.

And thinking will never help you overcome fear. Action will.

In order to live life to the fullest, you need to learn HOW to move past your fears. And that's the main focus of this chapter. Below mentioned are some of the most effective ways to banish any fear that's holding you back.

How To Overcome Your Fear?

These are the tools that I found to make the biggest positive impact against fear. I would like to share them with you now.

I came up with this list after reading hundreds of books, listening to audio programs, watching videos, attending seminars on fear, and testing their effectiveness on myself and other people.

Some of these techniques are backed up by real-world research, while some are old 'words of wisdom' that proved to be extremely helpful in real life.

So let's start with the first.

1. Mental Practice

Mental practice is an extremely effective way to banish anxiety and fear. Suppose you are afraid of going up to your boss and ask for a raise. Whenever you think about the scenario you imagine his frowning eyes, tensed lips, and "about-to-burst" vibe.

This creates anxiety in your mind. The actual scenario hasn't happened yet, but you imagined it would go badly.

There has been a lot of research done in this area in the last few decades. It has been found that the mind cannot tell the difference between real life and something imagined in detail.

As you imagine bad outcomes (i.e. your boss getting angry at you for asking for a raise) your mind responds as if it happened in the past. Consequently, fear is created to prevent you from doing that again.

The anxiety cycle goes like this:

Negative outcome imagined--> mind believes it --> fear & anxiety is created.

We need to break this cycle and turn it around so it helps us get what we want.

Let's take the same 'asking for a raise' example.

The night before you meet your boss, imagine you are walking into your boss's cabin with a smile on your face. Your boss greets you warmly. You start out with a friendly chat, then in a very relaxed, confident manner tell him that you think you deserve a raise.

Your boss looks receptive to the idea. You show him your last year's performance data and information on the current market value of someone with your experience. Your boss looks at the data you provided and agrees.

You exchange some pleasantries, shake hands, and walk out triumphant.

If you repeat this imagination several times, your mind will start believing it as truth. Your anxiety will completely banish or get reduced to a minimum. You will have a much stronger belief in a positive outcome.

Best of all, when you go up to your boss, you'll feel like you have done this several times before and the positive outcome has already happened. You will feel a lot more confident and self-assured. Other people (in this case, your boss) will really feel your positive energy and confidence and you will have a much higher chance of getting success.

This is called MENTAL PRACTICE.

It is a thoroughly researched and proven way to eliminate fear & anxiety and improve the performance of an individual. Now we know that the subconscious mind cannot differentiate between real and imagined, we can use it to our advantage.

If we imagine doing an activity repeatedly, the mind starts to accept it as a real-life event and records it in our memory. The more you repeat it in your mind, the better you 'adjust' to it in real life. This has a tremendous impact on fear.

If you repeatedly imagine - doing something you fear and obtaining a positive outcome from it, your fear will gradually disappear or get reduced to a minimum.

It was believed that the human body cannot run fast enough to cover a mile in four minutes. Nobody in history was able to do it. As a shocker for the medical world, Robert Banister was able to run a mile in less than four minutes.

When he was asked how he prepared for it, Robert said he regularly imagined running a mile under four minutes. He couldn't do it in the real world, so he did it enough times in his mind.

This removed the limitations and fear of failure from his mind. He completely believed that he would be able to do it and his body got him through.

That is one of the most inspirational stories I know that proves mental practice can eliminate fear and improve your performance.

And the best of all, it is very easy to do and requires nothing but a few minutes of your time.

How To Do Mental Practice?

1. Take something you really are afraid of (I.e. Public speaking, being rejected, failure in business, etc.)

2. Find a quiet, comfortable place.

3. Lie down and close your eyes.

4. Take 5-10 deep breaths. Relax your body.

5. Now start imagining yourself doing the activity. See yourself doing a good job at it. People are smiling at you. You are feeling confident.

6. Next, see yourself succeeding in your goal. You have achieved your outcome (I.e. you got the raise, your business is bringing lots of profit, you gave an extraordinary speech, etc)

7. Try to imagine it as vividly as you can. Try adding sounds, lights, color, touch, and feelings to your imagination.

8. Immerse yourself in your imagination emotionally. Really FEEL good about it.

9. Continue for 5-10 minutes.

That's it. This simple exercise has made a tremendous impact on my life as well as the lives of several people I know. Please use this exercise daily. You will start noticing a reduction in your anxiety within the first few days.

For a more permanent solution to fear & anxiety, combine mental practice with the below.

2. Face Your Fear

A friend of mine used to be terrified at the thought of speaking in front of the audience. We were doing an MBA together and all of us had to give a presentation on a pre-selected topic. I still remember, a night before giving his first presentation, he was very nervous.

I tried telling him that there is nothing to be afraid of. But it was of no use. Emotions tend to override logic every time. The next day, he was very nervous, literally shaking on stage. He fumbled his words, had poor eye contact, and was not engaging at all.

People in the audience felt bad for him because he normally was a friendly guy with a sharp mind.

After this not-so-great first experience, my friend was determined to get this handled, but he was still afraid of speaking on stage. Fortunately for him, as MBA students, we were called to give presentations again.

This time, I told him about mental practice. He was receptive to the idea. After doing some mental practice at night, he went to college the next day looking a bit more confident.

This time, my friend looked less afraid on stage than before, and when we pointed it out to him afterward, he felt even better.

In the next several presentations he gave, his fear gradually kept diminishing. All of a sudden, he was starting to speak louder, displaying confident body language, being more expressive, and engaging as a speaker.

Till the end of the two year period, he became one of the best in college at presentations.

This experience taught me that exposing yourself repeatedly to your fears actually lower their intensity. Is my friend still a little nervous before going on stage?

Yes.

But he has done it so many times, it now feels more like excitement than fear. He says, "exposing yourself to your fear takes the sting out of it and makes it quite manageable."

This is a thoroughly researched phenomenon. Read 'face the fear and do it anyway' by Susan Jeffers. It's an excellent book on this topic.

3. Having A Strong Faith

Faith and fear cannot coexist in your heart at the same time.

Have strong faith in yourself, your vision, and the ability to succeed. It is the light that guides you through the darkness. It's all about believing. You don't know HOW it will happen, but you know it will.

Every man on earth is created equal. The richest and most successful people have the same mind and physical structure as you have. Nobody is cut from a different cloth.

We all have the same body, energy, and time. The basic foundation is similar for everyone. It's the way you use what you have been given that makes all the difference.

Successful people use their resources on things like reading, training, taking action, finding solutions, making progress, etc.

Using their resources in a positive direction is what separates the best from the rest.

So believe in yourself and all that you are. Realize that there is something inside you that is greater than any obstacle. Right now, at this very moment, you have all the resources to become the person you want to be. You are more than enough, this very moment.

Think BIG!

Go for your desire!

Have UNSHAKABLE faith!

Faith is about noticing the mess, the emptiness, and discomfort, and letting it be there until the light returns. Your faith, at any point, should never be anything less than unbreakable.

There are two reasons for it. 1) Nobody is cut from a different cloth. You have the exact same resources as the ultra-successful people. 2) A breakable faith is of no use at all.

You cannot control everything. Sometimes, you just need to relax and have faith that things will work out. Let go a little and let life happen.

The harder your goal, the stronger your faith needs to be. Your faith is only as strong as the test it survives. Big goals need more time and effort. They also contain harder challenges. In such cases, your faith gets tested several times!

"None of us know what might happen even the next minute, yet still we go forward. Because we trust. Because we have faith." - **Paulo Coelho**

When all else fails, you can come back to your faith to take shelter from chaos & uncertainty. It's like an oasis in the vast desert. It is your place of certainty and calm. Strong faith has the power to keep you going even when it seems like all the doors are closed.

Let your faith be bigger than your fears.

Faith and fear cannot co-exist together. They cancel each other out. In your mind, there is a place for only one - faith or fear. And you get to decide which one exists. Choose faith. You create both - faith and fear. You have complete control over their existence.

"Faith and fear both have you believing in something which you cannot see... You decide." - **Bob Proctor**

Believe in yourself and your vision. Have faith in your abilities. Without reasonable confidence in your abilities, you cannot be successful or happy. There is no other way. A lack of faith will make you weak and ensure that you quit at the very first sighs of difficulty and setback.

Have faith and keep moving forward. That is the right way. That is the only way.

How To Strengthen Your Faith?

a) Start with your "why"

What is the reason for which you want your goal? If your "why" is important enough for you, you will keep a much stronger level of faith. But the only condition is that your reason must be very important for you.

When your reasons are important enough, you cannot afford to lose. The level of your desire is determined by how strong your faith is. So think about your "why". Keep it in your heart always. Feel its importance.

Turn that flame into a fire. Keep increasing it till you won't even consider any possibility of it not happening.

b) Positive affirmations

Affirmations have been proven time and again to be very good for creating and maintaining faith. Your mind is a sponge. It starts to believe any thought which gets repeated on a frequent basis. Use this power to your advantage. Affirm what you want several times in a day.

For details on how to do affirmations correctly, check out chapter 3: The art of building self-confidence.

c) Past success

If you have achieved any kind of success in the past, you tend to have more belief in yourself. If you have been successful at anything, take time to remember how you thought, how you felt, and what you did.

Remembering past success in a positive light will create faith in your mind - "I have dealt with challenging situations before and have been successful. I will make it... this time as well."

d) Everyone is equal

Knowing that ultra-successful people are just like you, have the same abilities, similar challenges and energy will strengthen your resolve. Many successful people have started their journey from a very low position - being broke, unhealthy, no education, no support, etc.

If you are reasonably educated, healthy, and have enough resources to read this book, you have a good starting point. Make most of it.

e) Small progress

Your faith becomes stronger as you take action and start noticing some progress. People say they don't have enough faith to take action. They don't realize that as you take action and start seeing some progress, the flames of your faith & desire start burning much brighter.

With your increased faith, you take much more action which gets you even better results over a period of time, which further increases your faith. It's like a continuous, upward cycle of strengthening faith.

f) Faith in God/Universe

Another strong source of faith is the feeling that some greater force is watching over you and if you give your best, you will be repaid. Religious people think of such greater force as God. If you are an atheist, you can think of it as the greater good or the universe.

Faith in some other greater entity will make you a bit relaxed and calm. When you believe there is a sense of justice in the world and your efforts are being taken into account, you won't be too worried about the result. You will do your best. You will honestly do your best.

"Your duty is to make your best effort, without worrying about the result... result will come." - **Lord Krishna**

When you honestly did your best... you will know. There will be peace in your mind. At that time, success or failure will not matter. You will feel like a warrior that has given it everything he had. It will be one of the most peaceful moments in your life.

Keep going. Keep moving ahead. Even if the result may seem impossible right now, keep it up. You will be pleasantly surprised.

This is it.

People are amazed at how something so simple, can be so powerful. If you are dealing with fear & anxiety in any area of life, use these ideas. Implement them in your thoughts. Make them part of your day.

But most of all - keep going forward. You can do it. You will do it.

The world will see your triumph.

I believe in you.

Keep going.

CHAPTER 3
THE SUBTLE ART OF SELF-BELIEF

Self-confidence is a superpower. Once you start believing in yourself, things start happening. Changing the way we think is a huge undertaking, and it really pays off in the end. If you take any kind of action without the necessary self-beliefs, it would be like driving a car with handbrakes on. It results in a lot of wasted energy.

You want to have your beliefs help you move forward, not slow you down. When you believe you can, you are halfway there. Once you win the battle in your mind, you will almost certainly achieve it in the real world.

We are going to cover everything now - what beliefs are, why are they important, how to identify negative beliefs and convert them into positive ones.

What are beliefs?

A belief is your sense of certainty about something. That's all. If you are CERTAIN about what something means, you have a belief about it.

There are two kinds of beliefs: conscious and subconscious.

The beliefs which we can NOTICE in our mind are conscious beliefs. We are aware of them. If someone asks you to write them down on a piece of paper, you can easily do it. For example, I am a good cook, I can dance well, I am a good person, I help people, etc.

On the other hand, some beliefs are buried deep below our awareness. We cannot articulate them, but we can "feel" their effect. Let's look at an example. Kamal, a friend of mine, was a naturally expressive guy when he was among his friends. But anytime he found himself surrounded by a few unknown faces (like in a party), he felt "fear".

Now, it's completely normal for people to have little social anxiety, but this was something else. His face would become red and his palms sweaty. He felt threatened and wanted to get out of the situation as fast as possible.

He started taking therapy sessions and, after one year, he discovered the cause of this fear. Actually, when he was a little boy, his family went to attend a large carnival. There were thousands of people at that carnival.

He accidentally got separated from his family and got lost in the crowd. As a little boy, it was a very scary experience. He was getting pushed by oncoming waves of unknown people. Some were looking at him weirdly. Some people tried talking to him which made him even more terrified.

He was later found by the security and taken back to his family. He was fine, but after this fearful experience with unknown people, his subconscious mind formed the belief that "strangers are dangerous".

And he had been carrying this belief deep within his mind ever since, and it really hampered his social life. At the age of 32, he could not articulate WHY he felt fear. He only knew that social situations scared him.

But, after therapy sessions, he was able to uncover the hidden subconscious belief and remove it from his mind. Later, in this chapter, you'll discover ways to find your own limiting subconscious beliefs and how to remove them from your mind.

For now, let's return to the current topic. We all have many conscious and subconscious beliefs about different things in life.

Even now, you have beliefs about who you are (as an individual), how other people are, and what you deserve out of life. This applies to all areas of life: relationships, money, business, health, body, mind, etc.

In each of these areas, you have different beliefs that govern how successful you'll be in that particular field. This is true not only for you but for everybody. We all are confined by our beliefs. Research shows the amount of success an individual can have, depends MASSIVELY on where he "believes" his limit to be.

Let's take an example of people who suddenly win the lottery. Maybe they won a million dollars, but somehow they spend all that money and return to the condition they were in before they won the lottery.

This is a powerful example of limiting belief in action. These people subconsciously believe they do not deserve to have a million dollars, so they always find a way to spend it and return to their old condition.

"Beliefs create the actual fact." – **William James**

Top experts and coaches of the world like Anthony Robbins & Brian Tracy get you to change your beliefs so that they help you succeed instead of blocking you.

Further, both conscious & subconscious beliefs can be of two types: positive beliefs and negative beliefs. The beliefs that help you to reach your goals are called positive, and the ones that block you from getting what you want are called negative (or limiting) beliefs.

We want to identify and eliminate negative beliefs that are stopping us from becoming the kind of person we want to be and install positive, empowering beliefs that move us towards our goals.

This is critical because our beliefs affect the level of ACTION we take. If you have negative beliefs then your mind will come up with hundreds of reasons why you'll never succeed and why it's better to give up right now.

On the other hand, having positive beliefs will be like having an internal coach, pushing you to move forward, regardless of the challenges you face.

Beliefs also affect your motivation levels. Positive beliefs provide certainty that you WILL reach your objective. That gives a big boost to your motivation.

And, just like action, motivation is also HINDERED by the presence of negative beliefs. A negative belief makes you think all the effort you are applying will eventually go to waste because you'll never reach your goal anyway.

As you can tell, beliefs play a very important part in achieving our objective of becoming a person with a positive mindset. It is critical that we get our beliefs to help us instead of stopping us from changing.

How your current beliefs are formed?

The majority of beliefs are formed during childhood when the brain is learning the ins and out of the world. And because the environment is so random, a child's brain forms the beliefs according to the conditions he is in.

For example, if a child grows up in a society where there is a lack of money, her brain is likely to form a belief that money is scarce and is something that is very hard to come by. On the other hand, a child who grows up in an abundance of money forms beliefs that money is abundant and easy to come by.

The surprising thing is the randomness of all this. Your negative and positive beliefs could be formed based on the environment you are in. It is completely random.

But here is the good news, you can change your beliefs at ANY point. When I started out, I had to change many of my negative beliefs and replace them with positive ones. It made a huge difference in the amount of success I had and my overall experience of life.

If you change your beliefs first, changing the action is much easier. Let me share a personal experience. When I was in high school, my elder sister gave me a pair of sunglasses. They were very nice and looked good on me. But I didn't wear them to school, because I believed I wasn't "cool enough" to wear them.

Just normal sunglasses.

We don't become what we want. We become what we believe.

Beliefs change how we look at the world. Your reality is a reflection of your beliefs. They act as lenses from which we look at the external world and create its meaning. In the presence of positive beliefs, your outlook will be more positive. You will be able to find something positive even from a seemingly bad situation.

And in turn, negative beliefs will make you focus more on the problems, obstacles, and reasons why you should not even attempt to do something about your situation.

If you pay attention, then you can easily find people around you who have positive beliefs. We all have at least a few people who have a positive outlook on the world. These people are optimistic and full of energy.

I highly recommend you stick close to these people as much as possible. Because beliefs, like emotions, are CONTAGIOUS. The more time you spend with these people, the more your outlook will change to be positive.

"You are the average of the five people you spend the most time with." - **Jim Rohn**

You will start feeling enthusiastic and, most importantly, begin believing that you can achieve your dream life.

IMPORTANT: Don't be discouraged if you can't find positive people to hang out with. I discovered that great books, audio, video programs, etc., all count towards changing your mind to be positive. It's not only about the surrounding people. It's about the top five "influences" that affect you on a daily basis.

Reading a book by someone who is massively successful WILL influence your mind to think like them. As you continually read, watch or listen to top individuals, you will gradually begin to adopt their beliefs and mindsets, which would be REALLY helpful if you can't find people like that in your actual life.

How beliefs are created?

Remember our earlier discussion that beliefs are something you are REALLY certain about? Well, to get that certainty, we require "evidence" that those beliefs are true. These pieces of evidence are called references.

An example of a reference could be your boss giving you props for completing a report on time. This recognition provides evidence for the belief, "I am competent at my work."

The more references you have, the stronger the belief would be. For example, if a beautiful girl has been getting praise for her beauty since childhood, she will have thousands & thousands of references proving that she is beautiful. Now the belief would be so strong that she doesn't need to even think about it. It is certain in her mind -- she IS beautiful.

Imagine your beliefs like a table-top, and references are the legs of the table. Without legs, the table cannot stand on its own. That's exactly how your beliefs work. References create and hold beliefs together.

If you remove the legs (or even weaken them), the table-top will fall. Similarly, collecting many pieces of counter-evidence for a belief will weaken it and eventually remove it from your mind.

This is a very powerful concept. It gives us insight into how our beliefs work and how they can be changed.

If you want more details on how references shape our beliefs, read the book Awaken the Giant Within by Anthony Robbins. It's one of my favorite books on the subject of NLP and beliefs.

Now, we will use what we have learned to create positive, empowering beliefs, while removing negative beliefs from our mind.

Effective ways to change your beliefs

1. Collect references that reinforce your positive belief

One of the most powerful ways to weaken your limiting beliefs while simultaneously strengthening a positive belief is to DELIBERATELY collect references for it.

To do this, think about two or three positive beliefs that will benefit you the most. These are the beliefs that you believe will be most helpful to have in your present situation. Now, take a new diary and write these beliefs down on the first page.

This is your table-top or the beliefs you want to have. Now you need to collect references (real-life evidence) to support your selected beliefs.

I would like to share a powerful secret with you. Your subconscious mind (where the beliefs are stored) does not give a damn about reason or logic. It never debates whether something is RATIONAL or not.

If you provide enough references, it will believe ANYTHING! You have the potential to have any belief you want in your life.

Now, as you go about your day, keep an eye out for anything which could even REMOTELY support your selected beliefs. For example, if one of your selected beliefs is "I am becoming a millionaire", then references to support that belief from your daily life could be:

a) I am always on time, just like a millionaire who is punctual. I am going to be one.

b) I worked the best I could today, just like the millionaires do. I have what it takes to be a millionaire.

c) I have a dream to be a millionaire, and I am working in that direction, just like self-made millionaires did. I am like them. I am going to be one.

A more suitable example would be – selecting a belief that "I CAN change myself to become a more positive person."

As you go about your day, consciously try to look at things in a more positive light. Even the smallest of incidents where you had a positive thought, counts as a reference of belief "I CAN change myself to become a more positive person."

Now, a very important part is to write down these references on a piece of paper or even on your mobile phone notepad. You are creating a written list of "references." Do not underestimate the power of written words.

When you go to sleep at night, take out your list of references you made during the day and look at it for a few minutes. Now you are seeing REAL WORLD evidence of positive thoughts that came in your mind during the day. It MASSIVELY boosts your self-confidence and strengthens your belief "I CAN change myself to become a more positive person."

In order to change, your mind craves proof (references) that you can become that type of person. And nothing could be more effective than a list of "real world" references that you collected during the day.

This list could be limitless. It only requires creativity and a positive approach. Any small, trivial thing could be your reference. You could even change the meaning of something negative and view it as a reference for your empowering beliefs.

For example, you want to start your own business but are doing a 9-to-5 job to pay your bills. If you are feeling bad about the current situation, you can change its meaning from "this is such a horrible situation. I am stuck here." to "You know what? This horrible experience is the universe's way of forcing me to work harder towards my goal: to create my own business."

You can change the meaning of any situation and view it as a reference to strengthen your empowering beliefs. Many people do it subconsciously... but they do it to reinforce NEGATIVE beliefs such as "people are mean", "money is hard to come by" or "I am not capable".

You will do it consciously... for the positive ones. As you find (or create) references during the day, write them down immediately on your mobile so you don't forget them. When you come home, WRITE THEM DOWN in your diary as "evidence for belief..."

Writing down your thoughts on paper works like magic. It penetrates deep in your mind. Your collected references will create a deep sense of certainty about your selected belief.

As you continue to collect references for your beliefs, within 4-5 days, you will start feeling different. The belief will begin to feel VERY REAL.

If you continue to gather references for your empowering beliefs (which you should), they will become so ingrained in your mind that nothing will ever shake them out. You'll have rock-solid beliefs for the whole life.

2. Affirmations

Affirmations are positive statements that you repeat again and again to fill your mind with absolute certainty. In our daily life, we are constantly bombarded with countless messages from media like TV, newspapers, and magazines that we are not enough, we'll never be as good as "them", we can't have that, etc.

Do you remember the TV commercial with a young, handsome guy with six-pack abs surrounded by six girls, or a female model with a perfect figure walking down the red carpet, or a celebrity arriving at a hot party in his Lamborghini?

While being completely harmless on the surface, this kind of exposure creates self-doubt in normal men and women about themselves. It subtly creates a "standard" in the minds of people which they believe they could NEVER reach.

What this does is to lower our confidence in ourselves and our capabilities.

And we need to fight against it. We need to RECLAIM our confidence and self-esteem.

This is where affirmations can help greatly. Affirmations will act as a daily reminder of your capabilities and your value as a person. It will be your daily "boost" of confidence. It will protect your confidence against all sorts of BS thrown at you.

Incredibly successful people like Oprah Winfrey, Will Smith, Jim Carrey, Arnold Schwarzenegger, and Lady Gaga swear by the effectiveness of affirmations.

Affirmations really do work, but you have to use them correctly. I have been doing affirmations for four years now, and I can honestly say they made a significant positive impact on my life.

How to do affirmations correctly?

1) Write down your doubts and insecurities on a piece of paper. Then, identify five of your BIGGEST doubts and insecurities which you believe are holding you back the most.

2) After you have identified five of your biggest doubts, write down their exact opposite positive statement. For example, if your doubts

statement is "I don't deserve to be rich", then its opposite positive statement could be "I fully deserve to be rich".

Change all five of your doubts into their opposite positive statements. Write them down on paper.

Note: Make sure all your affirmations are positive and in the present tense. Don't make affirmations for the future, like - I will succeed in the future, I will have a fit body, etc. your mind puts these statements in "maybe in the future" category.

Your affirmations must be positive and in the present tense. Example: I am successful, I deserve to be rich, I have a fit body, I have abundance in my life. Got it? Positive and present tense.

3) Now, after you have converted your five negative beliefs into positive ones on paper, write down another five Positive beliefs which you believe will help you the most. These five beliefs are the mindset which you would want to have. For example, I am a good learner, I can deal with any situation, etc.

4) You now have 10 affirmations that you would like to have as beliefs. Five positive ones converted from your negative beliefs, and another five which you think are great to have. It's time to install these 10 beliefs in your mind. Stand in front of a mirror (preferably full length where you can see your whole body) and look DIRECTLY in your eyes.

5) Say your affirmations out loud. Make sure to say them with PASSION & EMOTION, like you really believe them. You can use

your facial expressions and gestures to bring up the emotions while saying your statements. This is important.

For example, if your affirmation is - I am going to be a millionaire, say it like you REALLY mean it! Change your posture. Stand tall, chest forward like you are proud of yourself. Put both of your hands up and shout "YESSSSSSSSS!" in a triumphant voice. FEEL the emotion and passion in your voice. Now repeat your affirmation two more times.

Do whatever you can to bring emotion into your affirmations. Statements mixed with emotions have a deep penetrating effect on our minds.

Anthony Robbins (success coach, author of "Unlimited Power" & "Awaken The Giant Within") and Dr. Joseph Murphy (author of the bestselling book 'the power of your subconscious mind) stress the importance of mixing emotion in your affirmations. Without it, you would be doing affirmations for years without any benefit.

Do your affirmations daily. It only takes about 5 minutes, and within 2-3 weeks you will start noticing changes in your behavior. If you keep doing it, these positive statements will become a permanent part of your mind.

I personally used this technique to change my beliefs and it has worked amazingly well. It only needs a commitment from your part. Don't think about whether it will work or not. Suspend your disbelief and do it for a period of time. When you start noticing the difference, you would never want to stop.

3. Visualization

Visualization is a fancy word for 'vivid imagination' or 'imagined in great detail'.

It's a very effective technique for changing your beliefs. Medical science proved that the human mind cannot differentiate between something vividly imagined and real life.

In an experiment, researchers have placed scanners on the body of an athlete and got him to imagine running on a track in as much detail as possible. Scanners revealed that during visualization, his muscles were activating in the same manner as when doing the actual, physical activity of running on a track.

Since then, multiple researchers have verified the positive effect of visualization on the actual performance of an individual. Now, this fact is widely accepted in sports psychology and trainers put a huge emphasis on regular mental practice along with physical ones.

Now, here comes the interesting part - we know how beliefs are created and reinforced by 'real-life evidence'.

By using visualization, you can provide your subconscious mind any piece of "evidence" you desire because it CANNOT tell the difference between real life and something imagined in detail.

You can vividly imagine a scenario, and your mind will accept it as true. What this essentially means is that you can "manufacture" evidence that will reinforce positive beliefs in your mind.

This is a very powerful concept and its possibilities are virtually unlimited. For example, suppose you have social anxiety. You feel nervous about going to a party and talking to people you don't know. If you visualize for 10-15 minutes that you're in a party full of strangers and are feeling relaxed & calm while socializing with them, your mind will soon accept it as truth and your social anxiety would decrease by a good amount.

I personally used visualization to get rid of my fear of public speaking. In the past, I had some pretty bad experiences with public speaking. I used to stutter my words, lose my train of thought, wondering what people are thinking about me while standing on stage. It was pretty embarrassing.

But when I found out about visualization and how it works, I decided to give it a try. So, on a night before my big presentation, I closed my eyes and visualized giving a speech in a room full of people.

I felt the same anxiety as when I stand on stage in real life. It was pretty much the same feeling. But, I forced myself to deliver my speech as best as I could. As this was in imagination, whenever I messed up, I stopped & repeat it again and try to do it correctly this time.

It took 15 visualization tries for me to lose almost all of my anxiety while delivering my speech.

The next day, when I actually got on stage, it felt quite familiar. As if I had done it before. I did feel 'some' anxiety but it was quite manageable. My speech went quite well and people came up to me afterward to tell me how clear I was with my message.

Since then, I became a firm believer in the power of visualization. I used visualization in many other areas and it always helped.

Anthony Robbins, Brian Tracy, Jack Canfield, Donald Trump, Napoleon Hill, Zig Ziglar, Dale Carnegie, and countless other extremely successful people firmly stand by the power of visualization.

The best classic books like- Think and grow rich, See you at the top, Power of your subconscious mind, How to win friends and influence people, etc - recommend visualization as a tool to reach your goals faster.

On a personal note, the best resource I have found on the topic of visualization is Dr. Maxwell Maltz's book, Psycho-cybernetics. It has helped millions of people change their life for the better. I highly recommend checking it out.

Visualization is a very powerful technique but you have to do it correctly. Follow this simple, step by step method.

How to do visualization correctly?

1. First, sit or lie down in a relaxed, quiet environment. Make sure there are no distractions like excessive noise or lights. You should feel relaxed in this environment. For most people, such a place would be their bedroom.

2. Close your eyes. Take a few deep, relaxed breaths. Consciously relax your body and mind.

3. Once you are feeling relaxed, close your eyes. Start imagining that you have reached your goal. You have achieved what you wanted and now are filled with excitement & joy. Imagine it in as much detail as possible. It should be easy because it's something you really want. You will start feeling really good.

Note: Don't worry. You don't have to do it perfectly. Just add as many details as you can. After little practice, you will be able to visualize in much more detail.

4. Now keep viewing that vision (and feeling good) for few moments (1 to 5 minutes).

5. Open your eyes and relax.

That's it. Visualization is a very simple process (quite relaxing too) but its effects are AMAZINGLY powerful. I wholeheartedly recommend visualization to condition your mind for success.

Practice it daily. Preferably, once after getting up in the morning and once before sleeping at night. It takes only 5-10 minutes and is very effective for obtaining success in ANY area of life.

It's up to you now

By now, we have covered beliefs and their significance. We also covered three effective ways to develop positive, empowering beliefs. Use these tools effectively to strengthen your self-belief.

CHAPTER 4
STOP YOUR NEGATIVE THOUGHTS, FOR GOOD

a) Avoid negative people

People – who you surround yourself with – have a TREMENDOUS effect on your mind. It's a well known psychological fact that your thoughts and behavior are a combination of personalities of five people you spend the most time with. These 'five people' can be real people – friends, family, coworkers... or influences – books, television, internet sites, newspapers, etc.

Your mind is very receptive. It learns fast! These influences can be very beneficial or very harmful to you. If you spend most of your time among negative people who always put you & your abilities down, you would never feel confident. If your friends always whine and complain about things, you would end being a complainer as well.

Let me share a personal experience... Some time back, I landed a nice paying job in a good company. I thought everything was great. The atmosphere was good, people were friendly and the work profile was great. During the same period, I wanted to start an online business and was working on my blog.

My office hours, fortunately, gave me time to work on my online business, but... I did nothing. I didn't take any action despite all the free time I had. I always found some 'excuse' to delay the work.

As time passed, I started feeling bad for ignoring my heart's calling.

Soon, self-pity increased to a point where I couldn't take it anymore. I decided to figure out what was preventing me from taking action. For the next ten days, I observed my behavior very carefully and found that I had developed a crazy habit of making excuses.

I was not only avoiding my online business but also putting off office work and daily household chores.

It was unnatural for me because I never shied away from doing work. When did I start behaving like this? How did I form this habit?

I looked around and found that five of my teammates at the office were always trying to keep the workload as low as possible. They dreaded the thought of being burdened by work and were always making excuses to avoid it.

On an average day, I worked with them for the majority of my eight-hour job. My mind automatically picked up their 'excuse-making' habit.

The power of social influence is astounding.

Constant, repeated statements from surrounding people have the power to brainwash you. For example, a person who grew up in a family where people always say "money doesn't grow on trees" or "rich people are greedy" will have a very negative view of money.

Always remember, ANY kind of message that's constantly repeated to you (or around you) will enter into your thinking process. You will find yourself automatically thinking and behaving accordingly.

I did two things to reverse the damage. First, I got my seat shifted to a different place, bit away from them. Second, I started taking a huge amount of action daily to break the excuse-making habit. It was tough. It took me almost three months to get back to my normal behavior.

Be very careful when selecting people to spend time with. You will unknowingly CATCH their habits, thinking, behavior, talking & dressing style. You will become LIKE them.

Bottom-line: Reduce (or even completely eliminate) your interactions with negative, toxic people who bring you down. I honestly believe it's better to be alone than in bad company.

The good news is - it works another way around too. If you spend most of your time in the company of positive, successful people, or read their books, watch their videos, listen to their tapes... you will automatically internalize their thinking and behavior.

Positive influence doesn't need actual people themselves. It can be their books, audiobooks, videos, movies, songs... It all counts. Now you don't have an excuse to say "but I don't have resources to go and meet all those successful people".

Read their books, watch their videos...

It all counts in changing our mindset to a positive one.

b) Avoid instant gratification

As our society is progressing, we are constantly trying to make things easier, shorter & faster. The advancement in technology brought a new shift in our behavior. We have developed a deep fondness for quick fixes or magic pills.

Look at the commercials on TV today- "six-minute abs" or "the diet pill"

People are using drugs & alcohol to 'feel good'. In business, people are chasing 'get-rich-fast' schemes. In sports, athletes are getting caught using enhancements.

We want to feel good and successful, and we want it RIGHT NOW!

We live in an instant gratification society.

I believe there's a reason behind it. Ever since a child is born in our society, his/her mind is bombarded with instant gratification from all angles. Mom turns on the TV so kids can watch cartoons and don't annoy her with their request to play. From a very small age, we are exposed to advertisements, television, video games, fast food, and social media.

All of these are designed to make you feel good in short bursts. Once the 'good feelings' run out, you come back for more. Thus, becoming addicted to instant gratification.

Problems with instant gratification

There are several things wrong with instant gratification. To start, you lose good feelings the moment 'stimulation' ends. For example, if you are playing a video game and feel really good, just watch how it feels when you turn it off.

It's over, and you go back to feeling lousy the moment you return to the 'real world'. This fleeting nature of happiness makes you come back for more. It's like being on drugs. You want more and more and more...

Second, it distracts you from what really matters in the long term. People, who intend to lose weight, eat ice-cream because it feels good at the moment. People go and watch movies, instead of spending time together and having a meaningful conversation. People prefer to watch daily soap operas & filling their minds with drama instead of reading books. They go party when they should be working on their pending projects.

We want a short-cut to happiness and don't really want to put in the effort.

And, it never works.

I can't stress that enough.

True happiness & fulfillment come after you WORK on your heart's calling. Whenever I ignore any important work and do something meaningless (i.e. watch TV) to divert my mind, it feels really bad inside. It's like a constant, almost undetectable sadness. It makes the craving for instant gratification even stronger... which again leads to more internal pain and anxiety, which further intensifies the craving.

It's a negative cycle and something which you must break out of.

The first and the most effective way to break the instant-gratification habit is to realize that instant gratification can never make you happy. True happiness and satisfaction lie in TAKING ACTION towards your goals. When you move towards your heart's calling, you experience deep, long-lasting fulfillment.

Many people are afraid to take action. They fear being overwhelmed with work and challenges they may encounter. For them, it's like crossing a minefield.

In reality, nothing is further away from the truth.

Initially, you may resist doing your work, but I assure you... when you DO start, it will be the best feeling in the world. You will feel light. You will feel great. You will feel that this is THE most appropriate thing you could have done at this moment.

After you finish your work today, you will have a deep sense of satisfaction. You will laugh more. You will enjoy the simple pleasures of life which you would have ignored earlier. Little things will make you happy... because you are fulfilled inside. For today, the most important thing is done. You have finished your part.

Summary: Avoid seeking 'instant gratification'. The good feelings are temporary and will disappear quickly. Instead, follow your heart's calling. Put your best effort into it. You will experience long-lasting, REAL happiness & satisfaction.

CHAPTER 5
CONNECTION BETWEEN YOUR DIET AND MOOD

This is a big one! There is a saying - "*you are what you eat.*" The food you eat has a HUGE impact on your mood. Whenever we eat something, certain chemicals are released in the brain depending on the type of food consumed.

For example, consumption of omega-3 fatty acids - found in salmon, walnuts & kiwi fruit - supports synaptic plasticity in the brain and positively affects molecules related to learning and memory that are found in synapses.

Deficiency of omega-3 fatty acids may lead to shorter attention span, unstable mood swings, and even disorders like depression, dyslexia, and dementia.

Diets that are high in saturated fats are becoming recognized for reducing molecules that support cognitive processing and increasing the risk of neurological dysfunction. Link to research: www.ncbi.nlm.nih.gov/pmc/articles/PMC2805706

A lot of times procrastination, bad mood, feeling down, fear, anxiety, lack of concentration, and unclear thinking can be traced back to our unhealthy diet.

Let me share a personal experience. I used to eat heavy breakfast in the morning which included bread, milk, sprouted beans, eggs, etc. I thought it was quite healthy because it contained all the necessary nutrients. But, there was a small problem.

I just couldn't concentrate on work from morning till mid-afternoon. It was like being in a haze. My focus was all over the place. I couldn't think properly. I felt like a thick fog was covering my brain.

After reading a TON of books and online articles, I decided to switch to a green shake in the morning. It contained green leafy vegetables, nuts, essential oils, and some fruits. As you can probably guess - it tasted BAD at first, but I experimented with different fruits and got a combination that tasted really good.

Now for the important part- from the FIRST DAY I switched from heavy breakfast to a green shake, my mornings got completely transformed. My mind became extremely clear and focused. I could now properly concentrate on an activity without getting disturbed by random negative thoughts. I could now do the same amount of work in half-day that used to take me an entire day.

Sounds amazing, right? It was a revelation for me too. I always knew that healthy food was good for the body and mind, but never expected results to be this dramatic.

Watch what you eat. It makes a significant impact!

Basic Pointers for Maintaining Good Health and Mind

A. Eat clean

Think of food as fuel for the body, and you would want good quality fuel inside your body. Start by adding more fresh fruits and vegetables in your diet. Don't worry too much about cutting down bad foods. I found that if you start adding more healthy food in your diet, the quantity of bad food decreases automatically.

Reduce your sugar intake as much as you can. Stop eating fried, deep cooked, or barbecued foods. Try olive oil for cooking. It's a much healthier alternative to normal cooking oils. Make sure you are taking omega-3 oil as well, for its numerous benefits. Add a green salad with every meal. Eat foods with a low GI, which stabilize your blood sugar and provides energy all day long. Search "low GI foods" in Google for a big list of low GI foods.

Eat the right kinds of carbohydrates. Shift from simple carbs (white rice, white bread, white pasta, potatoes) to complex carbs (whole grain pasta, oatmeal, whole grain bread, vegetables, lentils), which break down slowly in the body, giving you a steady flow of energy throughout the day. You don't need much protein. The recommended amount is - 0.8 grams per kilograms of your body weight in a day. And while it's possible to get all the 20 different kinds of proteins entirely from plant sources (plenty of info available in books & the Internet), it'll be a bit tough. You can add a small amount of dairy or clean meats like chicken to your main fruits and vegetable diet. This will ensure that you get the whole range of amino acids easily.

If you eat a balanced diet with a wide range of fruits and vegetables, there will be enough vitamins and minerals included in your diet. Search online for the recommended quantity of vitamins & minerals per day. You should easily be meeting these requirements if you follow the guidelines above. If not, then consult your doctor for a good vitamin & mineral supplement. Sometimes it does wonders for your health and well being.

B. Drink enough water

Water makes up about 50-60% of our body. It is inside our cells, blood, tissues, and other parts of the body. A lot of body processes (like sweating) make us lose water fast. Sweating alone can use up to half-liter water in an hour. In extreme weather, that amount can rise to two liters of water consumed in an hour.

Even a 2% decrease in total water content level of the body, reduces our ability to perform at peak mental and physical level. If you continue to push on without drinking water, you will start getting irritable and tired, along with higher chances of getting muscle cramps.

A 5% decrease in the total water level of the body causes extreme fatigue and drowsiness. It may cause altered vision and tingling sensation in the whole body. 10-15% loss in water levels causes wrinkles on the skin and muscle malfunction. Any loss greater than that is often fatal.

Such is the importance of water for our health. Drink at least 2 to 4 liters of water daily depending on the weather conditions you are living in and the amount of physical activity you do. The more extreme the weather, the more water you need to preserve your water level. Drinking 2 to 4 liters of water is considered safe by many experts. Consult your physician to know exactly how much do you need based on your unique condition.

C. Exercise

It is quite well known that exercise is good for our health. Less known is the TYPE of exercise we need and its duration. Research shows that for most people a 15-minute brisk walk (walking at around 6 km/hr) is the ideal exercise, as it's not too stressful on the body and pumps up the oxygen flow nicely.

It is one of the few physical activities you can do your whole life. Even older people can take a brisk walk easily. The younger you start, the more benefits you get in the long term. No matter what your age, it's better to start exercising if you aren't already doing so. At a young age, the body can withstand heavy, rigorous physical activities. People in their 20s & 30s usually think about the gym and weight training whenever physical activity is mentioned.

For achieving optimum health, heavy exercises are not absolutely necessary. Here are some simple ones which are great for your health -

• Brisk walk

• cycling at slow speed

• sweeping or raking outside lawn

• gardening

• table tennis

• painting & plastering

• heavy house cleaning

• light dancing

• push-ups, sit-ups with moderate effort

It all depends on the effort you are willing to make and your physical condition. If you decide to take exercises like walking or cycling, one important point to note is you burn the same number of calories for covering a fixed distance.

For example, if you walk faster for 10 miles, you will burn a lot of calories initially but will slow down afterward. If you walk slowly, you will burn lesser calories but keep doing that longer.

In the end, whatever your speed is, you end up burning the same amount of calories for covering a fixed distance. As always, consult your physician before starting any new physical activity.

D. Adequate sleep

One of the most important things for your health is getting enough sleep. When you are well-slept, your mind is much sharper, alert, and resilient. You will have more energy, increased performance, and get a lot more done.

On the other hand, if you lack proper sleep, you will feel drowsy and irritable all day. Your willpower will decrease, emotions will be all over the place and become prone to instant stimulation which would eat up all your time. Sleep is one of those things which can either make or break your day. It is extremely important to get proper sleep at night.

But how much sleep is enough?

It depends on the individual. Every one of us is unique and has a different sleep requirement. Some people can function normally on 6 hours of sleep while others may need 8-9 hours to feel well-rested.

However, research on sleep shows that most people need 7 to 8 hours of proper sleep for optimum health and functioning. I personally need around 7.5 - 8 hours of sleep. When I sleep properly, I feel refreshed and energized all day.

Try getting up at different times in the morning to find your unique sleep requirement. You would eventually end up somewhere between 7 to 8:30 hours. Whatever your need is, get that many hours of sleep every day.

Don't be afraid of losing your productivity time. Some people think sleeping 8 hours is a waste of time. Actually, you will be a LOT more productive the whole day. You will get much more done.

That one hour of extra sleep will result in several hours of increased performance during the day. It's a worthy trade-off.

One more thing. It's not just the quantity of sleep which is important. "Quality" is also critical. Search online about improving the quality of your sleep. A lot of good information is available. Use that to your advantage.

Note: You should consult your physician before making any changes in your diet, exercise, or lifestyle. Each one of us has our own unique physical and mental condition and benefit from more personalized advice.

The pointers given above are general guidelines for good health, but professional medical advice should always be your priority.

Try switching to healthy food and notice the difference in your thought process. You will be pleasantly surprised. And if you continue with this diet over the long term, you will have better health and a strong immune system to boot.

CHAPTER 6
THE CLOSEST THING TO A MAGIC PILL

A healthy lifestyle not only changes your body, but it also changes your mind, your attitude, and your mood. Only a healthy body can sustain a healthy mind. And if you want your mind to be in its most resourceful, positive state... physical activity is a must.

Physical movement increases blood flow to all parts of the body, including the brain. It causes an increased supply of oxygen and nutrients which serve as fuel for the brain. A plethora of hormones are also released that play a part in sharpening cognitive functions in the brain.

In a recent study done by the department of exercise science at the University of Georgia, it was found that even exercising for 20 minutes lead to improved information processing.

And that's not all. Exercise also stimulates the growth of brain nerve cells (called a neuron) which support cognitive and behavioral brain functions.

What it means is, if you keep chilling out on your sofa all day, you are not giving your brain a chance to operate at its full potential.

Observe people who sit continuously for 8 hours in the office. They come home groggy, fatigued, and unable to think clearly. I used to be one of them.

When I was working in a corporate job, I could feel my mind going 'numb' after 2-3 hours of continuous sitting on the computer. I was not going to a gym at the time. It all added up and dropped my mental energy levels to a point that I didn't even want to talk to anyone. It was very tough to feel happy and enthusiastic about ANYTHING.

If you would have asked me to do any creative work, the only response you would have gotten was a 'blank stare'. There was just no way I could process complex tasks, be creative and enthusiastic.

Nope. None of that was possible.

After months of 'mind numbness', I finally decided to do something about it. I started reading about brain health and how it is related to physical movement.

I started small.

I started doing 20 minutes of light jogging in the morning AND getting up from my chair every 30 minutes during the day in my office. I basically added more 'movement' to my daily lifestyle.

The results were better than I expected. I started feeling better. My energy levels increased along with my mood and enthusiasm. I became more vibrant and involved. People in my office were surprised by the sudden change in my demeanor. Everybody started appreciating this new 'me'. I started getting lots of compliments from others (they probably wanted to motivate me to stay like this).

I never expected to have this much positive energy if I just moved around more. Frankly, it was quite surprising. I had read about how exercise PROVIDES energy instead of depleting it, but it's quite powerful to actually EXPERIENCE it yourself.

I maintained this lifestyle ever since. Now my morning routine consists of a 30-minute walk and 15-minute meditation. It gives me mental and physical energy which lasts all day.

I highly recommend taking a minimum of 30 minutes daily for physical activity - weightlifting, cardio, yoga, tai-chi, jogging, walking, cycling - select anyone you like. Do check with your doctor before starting.

In addition to the above morning exercise, get up from your chair every 30 minutes to stretch your legs. Take a short walk around the office. Go to the water cooler take a sip and come back. Just get up and move around a bit.

Try doing both of these for 10 days. You will notice a great improvement in your positivity and energy levels. It refreshes mind & body and adds more 'life' in your day.

And when you consider the long-term health benefits of this lifestyle, it's really a no brainer.

CHAPTER 7
WHAT WILL YOU CHOOSE?

A positive attitude gives you power over your circumstances instead of circumstances having power over you. It is a little thing that makes a big difference. It's not what happens to you, but how you react to it that matters.

I still remember when I used to read about the importance of a positive attitude and think - "yeah, yeah. Su...re"

Deep inside, I didn't quite believe in its importance.

Now after making an effort for thirteen years to change my negative mindset to a positive one, I am now completely convinced that a positive Attitude is EVERYTHING. Every thought we have is influenced by our attitude. Positive attitude reinforces positive thinking, which moves us in the right direction, while a negative attitude gives birth to negative thinking.

Why do you think one person has an optimistic outlook, while the other dwell in negativity? Both are quite similar in all aspects - education, age, culture, background, society, etc.

The only difference is in the attitude.

Whenever a positive person faces a challenge, his focus would be on finding a SOLUTION to the problem. It would be easy for him because he would imagine a bright future. He BELIEVES in a better future.

When a negative person deals with similar challenges, he would ignore the possibility of sunshine behind the mountain. He would focus on the negative - how bad things are, it's taking too much time, it's not going to work, and so on.

Happiness is an attitude. We can make ourselves miserable, or happy and strong. The amount of effort is the same.

Everyone has the potential to live a fulfilling life. The difference lies in how we look at things. When someone views the world as a horrible place, he or she has taken themselves out of the game before they even had a shot at happiness.

Life is just too short to be serious all the time. If you cannot laugh at yourself, call me... I'll laugh at you. All you can change is yourself, but sometimes that alone changes everything.

The Impact of a Small Shift...

The good news is, even a small shift in attitude can bring great results.

One of my friends used to struggle with being social in his office. He was an introvert by nature and had troubles opening up to new people. He always said, "I have nothing to talk about, and even if I did, they will not like me anyway." I sat down with him and convinced him to just say hello to people in his office and smile. He agreed because it was only a small shift in behavior.

The results were amazing. People were very receptive to his greetings and started conversations themselves. Initially, my friend was a bit nervous in conversations but it quickly became a habit. Now he is well known by his colleagues and has the reputation of a warm and social person.

A tiny shift in attitude gave such a great result.

In life, success and failure are only inches apart. A very small shift is needed to get either result. No matter how many mistakes you make or how slow your progress is. You're still way ahead of everyone who isn't trying.

Cultivate a positive attitude.

If you want more proof, look at people who are consistently at the top of their respective field - CEOs, successful entrepreneurs, world-famous actors, award-winning athletes, great singers, artists, and professionals who became icons of their generation - all have a positive attitude in life.

If you read the autobiographies of famous people, who are considered 'greats' of their field, the importance of attitude becomes apparent. Nelson Mandela, Steve Jobs, Albert Einstein, Mahatma Gandhi, Mother Teresa, and countless other great people's stories are proof that whatever your aim, a positive attitude will bring success and fulfillment, while negativity will lead to an inevitable downfall.

Your attitude determines your direction.

This is especially true nowadays. A positive attitude is very valuable. It gives you the resilience to face the harshness of life. You cannot always have a good day, but you can always face a bad day with a good attitude. No matter how big your problems get... if you look for the positive things in life, you'll find them.

The reverse is also true. Look around and you will find that people who are negative, usually wind up being miserable their whole lives. They lack gratitude and general satisfaction. Their relationships become toxic and eventually get destroyed.

We can say negative people are the "losers" in life.

And because attitude is contagious, you have to keep yourself away from negative people. We all have some negative, "emotional leech" types of people in our life. Each one of us knows a few, and it's best to keep your distance away from them as much as possible.

I have identified some people like that in my life and minimized my interactions with them. One of my friends introduced me to Raj. At first, I liked him, but later when I started hanging out with him, I realized he was constantly complaining about everything. He could find fault in everything & everyone. No matter how I tried to be normal around him, his strong negative outlook overwhelmed me every time.

Soon 'I' started pointing out faults in things, which I don't normally do. My other friends started telling me that I was changing. I was not positive and upbeat as before. Then I realized how strongly people influence each other. I minimized my interactions with Raj and decided to stay away from such an attitude as much as possible.

How to Develop a Positive Attitude?

Conversely, be near positive people. Watch how they talk, what they say, how they think. Expose yourself to positive people as much as possible.

It is a psychological fact that we become a combination of five people with whom we spend most of our time. Be around people who are successful, positive, grateful, and your mind will start adopting their behavior automatically. We subconsciously absorb the thinking of the other person, whether it is positive OR negative. That's the way our brains are wired.

"Associate yourself with people of good quality, for it is better to be alone than in bad company" - **Booker T. Washington**

What to do if you can't find positive people around you?

Don't be discouraged if you can't find positive people to hang out with. I discovered that great books, audio, video, programs, etc., all count towards changing your mind to be positive. It's not only about the surrounding people. It's about the top five "influences" that affect you on a daily basis.

Reading a book by someone who is massively successful will influence your mind to think like them. As you continually read, watch or listen to top individuals, you will gradually begin to adopt their beliefs and mindsets, which would be really helpful if you can't find people like that in your actual life.

One of the biggest advantages of having a positive attitude is that it changes your focus from "surviving" to "thriving". Have you noticed people who are just coping through life? Their whole motivation is to just "get by". For them, having just enough to survive is FINE.

With the right attitude, you will see situations and people differently. Your focus will be on what's good and what's possible. There will be aliveness inside you which other people will instantly notice. You will have more passion and zest for life because your dreams are ALIVE.

"Be the one thing you think you cannot do. Fail at it. Try again. Do better the second time. The only people who don't tumble at the high wire are those who never mount the high wire" - **Oprah Winfrey**

Imagine yourself on a boat in the middle of a lake. The boat is your attitude and the shores on either side are happiness and misery. If your attitude is right, you will move towards the shore of happiness. If you embrace negativity, you will move in the opposite direction, misery.

Some people ask me whether it is possible to change the course if you have been moving in the wrong direction. My answer: I firmly believe it's NEVER too late to change. You can always change at any point in your life.

There are countless examples of people who changed their destiny after the age of 50, 60, 70. It'll be a little tougher if you have been in a negative spiral all your life. But it is 100% POSSIBLE. Many people, exactly like you, have changed their life.

It's never too late...

Attitude change exercise

A great start would be to train yourself to find *one* good thing in people and situations. Just *one* is enough (but more is obviously better). If you find it hard, keep in mind that every bad situation will have something positive. Even a stopped clock shows the correct time TWICE a day.

Do your best at it. Pretty soon, it will become a habit.

In research done by the Harvard institute, researchers have found that technical knowledge is only fifteen percent of achieving success. The rest of the eight-five percent comes from having a positive attitude and thinking.

Be an optimist because there is not much use of being anything else. Positive thinking will let you do everything better than negative thinking will.

I believe that sometimes the bad times in our lives put us on a direct path to the very best times in our life. Whenever you feel discouraged or depressed, try your best to change your attitude. Ships don't sink because of the water around them. They sink because of the water that gets in them. Don't let what's happening around you get inside you and weigh you down.

Happiness is not by chance, but by choice... and it's all in the attitude.

CHAPTER 8
THE REAL SECRET TO HAPPINESS

Happiness starts with you. Not with your relationships, not with your job, not with your money, but with you. To experience true happiness and satisfaction, you need to stop relying on the outside world to make you happy. Happiness is living life from inside-out. We have to look deep inside ourselves to find a source of happiness that could never be depleted. I believe this inner source is made up of two aspects:

1) Self-esteem

2) Present to the moment

In my experience, these two traits form the source from which we can draw happiness infinitely. We never have to depend on our environment & people to feel happy. It does not mean we stop engaging with the outside world. For example, we can certainly enjoy watching movies and social interactions, but they are not the main source of our happiness.

Our main source of happiness is within us. Even if we are removed from external stimulation, we always have our inner source to go back to.

In this chapter, we are going to look at the first aspect: self- esteem. We will cover everything – what is it, why it is important, and how to increase your self-esteem?

What is Self-esteem?

Self-esteem is the value you have in your own mind. It does not matter what everyone else thinks about you. What's important is how you think about yourself.

Your self-esteem determines your self-respect, your confidence, your happiness, the amount of love you give to yourself and others, how you take care of yourself, how resilient you are, and your overall level of success in life.

Self-esteem forms the foundation for a life worth living. It affects EVERYTHING! Your success, relationships, health, perspectives, peace, and the amount of happiness you allow yourself to feel and your reactions to the various events happening in your life.

Benefits of High Self-esteem

- More joy & happiness

- More enthusiasm

- High energy levels

- Increase in confidence

- More authenticity

- Less social anxiety

- Wanting to achieve more

- More caring towards self and others

- Increased focus and concentration

- More socially adept

- Not comparing yourself with others

- Less fear and worry

There are many other benefits aside from mentioned above. The point is, self-esteem increases your quality of life more than anything else.

Effect of low self-esteem

- People having low self-esteem feel a sense of lack. An internal voice telling them that they are not enough.

- People feel bored and they lack energy. They are less likely to take good care of themselves and others. They are less likely to go to the gym, eat healthy food, and groom themselves properly.

- The willingness to achieve success goes away. They feel a huge surge of internal resistance when they think about taking action towards their goals.

- Low self-esteem people procrastinate a lot. They self sabotage themselves.

- Criticism from others has a big emotional impact. And the whole thing keeps repeating in their head all day.

- People with low self-esteem compare themselves with other people and always end up feeling inferior.

• Even if someone or something puts them in a fun mood for the moment, Low self-esteem people return to their negative, bored mood as soon as that fun runs out. They leech positive emotions from other people, which drive others away.

• Lousy relationship with other people. Low self-esteem hinders their ability to fully love and care about other people.

• Lesser emotional stability. A person with low self-esteem is likely to be angry, upset, enraged, cry, depressed easily than a person having high self-esteem.

• Low self-esteem causes a negative spiral. A Person already feeling down, does things like arguing with other people, procrastinate, eat a lot, does not take care of himself, etc. These things make him feel worse and his self-esteem gets even lower. This is the negative, downward spiral created by low self-esteem.

We want to have high self-esteem. How we can get it? And if we have low self-esteem, how do we break out of the negative, downward spiral and raise our self-esteem for a more fulfilling life?

How to raise your self-esteem?

1. Living up to your values

This is the single BIGGEST factor that determines your self-esteem. You have some values which are nothing but your ideals, goals, dreams, rules, aspirations, etc. To raise and maintain high self-esteem, it is critically important that you TAKE ACTION and MOVE TOWARDS your values.

Yes, I said to take action. You have to take action. High self-esteem is the result of taking action towards your values.

Furthermore, you have to take action daily. The ups and downs of self-esteem happen on a daily basis. It is crazy to think about, but on a day when I don't take any action and move closer to my values, I feel my self-esteem drop rapidly!

On the other hand, on the days when I do take action, my self-esteem soars high as well.

I strongly suggest that you get clear about what your values are, and then take action on a daily basis. It's all about personal integrity that comes from knowing that you are not lying to yourself by watching T.V. when you should be working on your pending project.

Sometimes, we have some values that clash with each other. For example, if two of your important values are FAMILY and WORK. You sacrifice spending time with your family because you are busy with work. You will have high self-esteem for a while but it will slowly start to fade as you continue to neglect to spend time with your family (Family Value).

The answer is to have a BALANCE. Do something for all of your priorities no matter how small that action would be. For this example, you could try to take out little time to spend with your family daily despite your work OR you promise your family that you all will go on a weekend trip and spend the entire weekend together without any distraction from your work. There is always a way to have a balance in your clashing priorities.

Taking action towards your values raises your personal integrity, which in turn raises your self-esteem.

This particular concept made the single BIGGEST impact on my self-esteem among all techniques mentioned in this chapter. Even if you do nothing else, just internalize this concept. You will be amazed by the increase in your self-esteem.

2. Take care of yourself

Another way to raise your self-esteem is to take proper care of your health and grooming. Go to the gym. Wear well-fitted clothes which look good on you. Eat healthy food that nourishes your body. Avoid junk foods. Get a better haircut. Take care of your skin and hair. Invest in yourself... both money and time.

When you are working hard in the gym or going the extra mile to shop for healthy food, your mind will realize that you value yourself. Your self-esteem will soar. The added effect will be that you feel much healthier and attractive because you have been taking care of yourself. On top of that, you will feel amazing due to high self-esteem because you took the pains to take care of yourself. You value yourself.

When you are in this kind of state, you will inspire people to do the same.

3. Stop comparing yourself with others

People with low self-esteem tend to compare themselves with other people. And usually, they end up feeling worse about themselves. This is because we only evaluate other people's apparent strengths we initially see... their looks, their money, their status, etc.

We have no idea about their weaknesses.

While we don't fully know them, we are completely aware of OUR weaknesses. We compare our weaknesses against their PERCEIVED strengths... and we end up short.

This whole comparison thing is complete nonsense. Our view is distorted. A person is never static. We are always changing... growing mentally, emotionally, financially, physically, spiritually. We have a vast number of unique traits. For example – our unique outlook, life experience, beliefs, body type, perspectives, likes and dislikes, how we can cook, how we love, how we write, what we dream, the way we live, our past, our friends, our family, our choices, and it goes on and on....

When we are made up of THOUSANDS of UNIQUE traits, and we are CONSTANTLY CHANGING and growing every moment... how can we determine our self worth by comparing 1 aspect of ourselves with the other person? Is it even possible? NO.

Remember, we are all unique. Our creator made each one of us special, and we were sent here for a purpose. That purpose is unique to each individual. So stop comparing yourself with others because it is not possible. Instead, accept yourself completely, then find your purpose, your mission, and work on it with all your heart.

You will be filled with a sense of integrity and high self-esteem.

4. Look for the good in other people

There is a lovely story about a boy who had a fight with his mom and went to a top of a mountain and shouted in the valley – "mom, I hate u... I hate you... I hate you..."

An echo returned from the valley – "I hate you... I hate you... I hate you..." The boy was startled. He ran back to his house and told his mom that there was a mean little boy in the valley that shouted at him – I hate you.

Mom smiled. She took her boy to that spot again and told him to shout again, but this time he has to shout – "I love you... I love you... I love you..." Boy did as she said.

To his surprise, now there was a sweet little boy in the valley shouting – "I love you... I love you... I love you..." His mom told him that when you love other people, they love you back.

The world works exactly like this. What you give out, you receive back 100 folds. If you give out love and care to others, you will get affection and support back. If you give out anger and hatred, you will receive the same in return.

It is really important to treat others well. When you treat others well, you feel good. And when they treat you well in return, you feel good. It's a win-win situation. But how will you start treating others well?

How you look at other people determines how you will treat them. For example, if you see others as basically good people, it is much more likely that you will treat them with warmth. On the other hand, if you see other people as self-centered, your behavior will be cold and standoffish towards them.

So always, always remember this golden rule of life:

Always ask yourself – what is good in this person? How can I find his/her good qualities?

When you ask this question, your mind will zoom in on the positive qualities of another person and you will look at them with admiration and warmth. Others will feel that and treat you similarly.

Man is a social creature. Our ability to form a community is our biggest strength. It is in our genes. When you treat others well, your self-esteem and personal integrity rise because you are living the way you were designed to be.

Now it's your turn.

All of these techniques are simple and can be done by anyone who's willing, and the return of benefits is much greater than the time & effort invested.

I urge you to use these methods to increase your self-esteem and stick to the ones which work best for you.

CHAPTER 9
FREEDOM FROM STRESS AND PRESSURE

We will now look at the second part of inner happiness – "Power of presence".

Emotions like fear & worry are prevalent in today's world. Some people say these emotions are imposed upon them by media, some argue that these are self-imposed. I think it is a combination of both.

The media does play a part but a major portion of suffering & negativity in our life is our own doing. We play a huge role in bringing emotions like fear, worry, guilt, anxiety, etc in our life. Let's see how, and what to do about it.

Thousands of years ago, Buddha said – *"Thoughts are the cause of all suffering."*

Our emotions are caused by the thoughts in our minds. If you are like the majority of people, your mind has become habitual of negative thoughts. Negative childhood experiences, toxic family environment, news, social media & advertisement are constantly conditioning your mind to never feel enough, never feel safe, and never feel good enough to be happy.

Negative thoughts create negative emotions. And you can never completely stop these thoughts. Even if you consciously try to get rid of the thoughts, it will not work. Thoughts will stop for a moment or two but return as soon as you put your attention elsewhere.

In the Buddhist culture, this is called 'monkey brain'. Your thoughts and attention wander like crazy. If you try to control them, you will never win.

However, at the same time, you cannot let your 'monkey mind' control you. You have to take control. The ultimate freedom is freedom from your thoughts. As long as you are being chained by your thoughts, you can never be happy & fulfilled.

Suppose you are trying to have a happy, carefree conversation with your partner at home and your mind is wondering about the project report you have to complete tomorrow before lunch. Can you see how handicap it makes you mentally?

Instead of being in the present moment and having fun, your mind is dwelling on the negativity which could 'possibly' happen in the future. How crazy is that? You are messing up your current happy moment by worrying about some negative things which you are not even sure will happen…

I was introduced to the concept of being in the present moment by book: *Power of now* by Eckhart Tolle. It made quite a difference in my outlook. It made me realize that emotions like fear & worry cannot survive in the present moment.

The mind needs either past to feel guilt & anger, or future to feel fear & worry. If you are focusing on what is in front of you at this very moment, you are completely engaged, completely content, and… completely free. There will be a deep sense of calmness in everything you do. When you get habitual of living in the present moment, you would feel a sense of peace underlying every experience, whether negative or positive.

Since then, I started seeking additional information about the presence and tried many different 'methods' & 'Systems'. Some worked well for me, some did not. Below is the list of most effective ways to cultivate present moment awareness that I have found.

How to live in the present moment

1- Meditation

The best way to become more present in your daily life is to practice meditation. Meditation trains your mind to be in the present moment. But realize that meditation is a daily practice. You cannot discontinue meditation after six months, thinking now you don't need it.

Mediation works exactly like going to the gym. When you keep doing it, you will feel increasingly more present to the moment in your daily life. When you stop, within a few days you will feel the difference. You will start to fall back into your old thought pattern.

Nothing is constant. What doesn't grow, starts dying. This applies strongly to meditation. Start doing meditation daily. Its benefits are much greater than the amount of time & effort you exert.

Now the main questions are – How long your daily meditation sessions should be & How to do meditation?

The Answer to the first question is – it depends upon you. I find 10 to 15 minutes of daily meditation enough. It makes me more present & calm in my day to day life.

Here is a simple, step by step guide for doing meditation effectively.

How to Meditate?

a) Set an alarm for 15 minutes.

b) Sit comfortably on a chair, keeping your back relaxed & upright. Use Cushion if you need to.

c) Close your eyes and start noticing your breath coming in and out. Notice everything about it: when it enters your nostrils to when it goes in your diaphragm. The movement of your stomach going up and down, etc.

d) Eventually, your mind will start thinking about something. You will get lost in your thoughts. You lose focus on your breath and start dwelling on the thought itself. It's Ok.

e) Whenever you catch yourself focusing on your thoughts instead of being aware of your breath, gently and calmly shift your focus to your breath.

f) What will certainly happen is you will lose your focus again and get lost in thoughts. Again, simply shift your focus to your breath calmly.

g) Keep doing this for 15 minutes till your alarm rings.

Note: Don't force yourself to keep your mind empty all the time. Your mind will think and that's what we want. Actually, your mind gets stronger when you shift your focus back from your thoughts to your breath. This back-and-forth of awareness is what strengthens your mental muscles. It's like a gym for your mind.

This simple exercise will increase the performance of your mind (i.e. clarity of thoughts, concentration, willpower, focus) to astronomical levels. Its effectiveness is unmatched. Studies all over the world are attesting the positive effect of meditation on our brain. I would even confess that I would not be able to finish this book if it wasn't for meditation.

Another KEY point related to meditation is consistency. It doesn't matter whether you meditate for 5 minutes or an hour, just make sure you are meditating REGULARLY. Because if you miss one day, you would probably find an excuse to miss the next day. Be consistent. Don't skip a day. If you are extremely busy, meditate for 5 minutes just before you sleep at night. Make it a regular habit.

It will not take long before you start noticing the positive effects of meditation (took me a month). And once you DO start seeing them, you would never want to stop meditating.

After my initial six months (of doing meditation), I stopped, thinking that effects must be permanent now. Within a week I noticed a sharp decline in my concentration, self-control, mood, and thought clarity.

When I am meditating regularly, I can easily focus on a single task for hours. Time flies by without me noticing. While writing this book, I was able to write continuously for four-five hours without getting distracted. I also found that I could ignore negative thoughts and fully concentrate on the end result.

Let me share another example. I really wanted to make my book *Success Habits of High Achiever*, the best possible resource anybody could find on the topic of success. But several times, negative thoughts would take over -

"Maybe it's not as good as I thought."

"Who am I to write a book? I have never done it before."

"It will never reach people who need it."

"It's a waste of time."

During this phase, meditation gave me internal strength. It helped me regain my composure and focus. I said to myself "No, it is good." and "There are people who need it and I'll make sure they get their hands on it."

I would even say that if it wasn't for meditation, I wouldn't be able to finish the book.

I highly, highly recommend taking 15 minutes of your time and do meditation. Its profound benefits will help you tremendously in ALL areas of your life.

2- Pay complete attention to the present activity

When doing your day to day activities, be more aware of the environment around you. Really look at things. I mean it. Really look at them. Notice small details like colors, shape, weight, taste, smell, shine, etc.

This will allow you to cultivate present moment awareness. When coupled with daily meditation practice, your mind will not wander. You will feel the difference. In about ten days, you'll start noticing things you ignored in the past because you are now paying attention.

Really looking and engaging in an activity will shut down your thoughts and time will seem to fly-by. Do you remember the last time you were engaged in your favorite hobby and hours went away like minutes? That was the power of being present in the moment.

Because you like that activity, you are paying your complete attention to it. You are present to the moment with no thoughts & worries. Time flies by. After you finish that activity, you feel energized and peaceful.

The good news is, when you learned to be in the present moment, you would feel like this after every activity you do.

3- Be aware of your thoughts

This concept is from a mindfulness meditation technique. You start paying attention to the thoughts that are going on in your brain, NON-JUDGEMENTALLY. Do not label any thoughts good or bad. Just observe them objectively. You will notice that thoughts are coming from a 'different' source.

It is not YOU who is thinking. Rather the thoughts are generating from somewhere else. You and your thinking mind are separate entities. This concept plays a very important role in allowing you to separate yourself from your thoughts.

You no longer identify yourself with your thoughts. You can clearly see that you and your thinking mind are different, so you stop taking ownership of your negative thoughts. It is not you who is thinking. You are a separate entity. So when you are different from your thinking mind, you have the option of not listening to your thoughts. You may hear them, but do not pay them any importance. This makes it easier for you to stop giving un-needed attention to your negative thoughts.

This may not be-all-end-all for being present but can be a great starting point. Try this one.

4- Minimize activities which stop you from being present

One of the best ways to be more present is to minimize activities that make your brain dull & unable to focus on the present. Some activities make you present and some don't. If you aim to become more present, then gradually remove activities that are not helping that goal.

Activities like watching TV, playing video games, drinking alcohol, taking drugs, etc are some of the ways people 'numb' their brain to the present moment. Instead of facing deeper issues, they try to find happiness by escaping reality.

What these people don't realize that running away from the present moment will never make them truly happy. They might feel good momentarily but they will never feel 'satisfied'. Running away will never solve anything. Only when you start embracing the present moment and face deeper issues, you will feel content.

What's so scary is that these activities are so deeply ingrained in our society that they are considered good... even luxury by some people. But since we intend to become more present to the moment, it is imperative that we gradually minimize or completely remove these activities from our daily life. It will allow your daily lifestyle to help you become present.

5- Make regular activities fun

When you spend time doing what you like, you become completely present to the moment. Your brain is getting pleasure from that activity and it reacts by paying full attention. Time seems to fly by & you feel amazing!

This is a natural phenomenon experienced by everyone engaging in their hobby. Hobbies are activities that are fun for you. This makes you like doing them. They make you completely present and focused on the now.

If this is so, then why not try to make every activity enjoyable?

While doing a bland activity, ask yourself – "how can I make this fun?" This question will put your focus on how to make that activity fun. When you are focused on making that activity fun (and start having fun) your mind will put complete focus on that activity because it likes to have fun.

Be creative with this. Try to make as many activities as you possibly can to be more interesting & fun. This will provide several benefits. You will be more in the present moment, more fun, life will feel more interesting and you will become much more engaged. Stress and worries will seem to disappear...

You will hit many birds with one stone. Talk about gaining returns for the small investment!

It is the journey that counts, not the destination.

Remember, no matter how bad it looks right now, this is the golden moment. You are in the process of changing yourself. In future - when you would look back - this would be the moment you will feel most proud of. This moment is the real reward. So enjoy it. This moment is all there is. When you see it that way, nothing, I mean nothing will be capable of touching you emotionally.

CHAPTER 10
STORMS DON'T LAST FOREVER

At times, you'll face a situation where you have to make some compromises. Sometimes situations will force you to change directions.

There will be instances where you would feel that you are drifting away from your path... the distance between you and where you want to be is increasing.

This feeling can be bad for your confidence.

All that effort you made till now feels 'wasted'.

It feels frustrating.

I completely understand. I have been through it myself.

It sucks. Really.

It feels BAD.

But let me share with you what I do to get out of this kind of situation.

First of all, don't stress over it anymore. What's done is done. No amount of stressing over it will help you in any way. In fact, stress hampers your abilities to think rationally and doing the right thing.

Completely accept the fact that you are going through a difficult time period. Do not resist the truth. The more you resist the truth, the more it will hurt. Accepting it will calm your mind. You will feel a lot in control of your emotions.

Yes, it would feel 'bad' to accept what has happened, but trust that the universe wants you to learn something new. It wants you to be stronger than you currently are. It increases your resilience, hardens your resolve.

Excluding the death of a loved one, everything is a part of the overall good. You may not feel it now but in the long term, it will benefit you. Trust me. Five years from now, when you will look back to this situation YOU WILL BE GLAD IT HAPPENED.

It's part of the overall good. Then, you will see this truth and share with others what I am sharing with you now.

For now, just accept the fact that you are going through a difficult time period. It will calm you. Then, focus your full attention on the present situation… What should you do now? How do you deal with it? What's the best course of action you can take from here?

But for this, you must have a calm mind. Acceptance of the present situation is necessary. If you are stressed, you won't be able to think rationally. Calm yourself.

Then, when you are in a calm headspace, keep moving forward. Do what you have to do now. Adjust to the new condition and try to see the good in it.

I know it's not what you originally wanted. You may feel that your life is moving in the wrong direction. But... have faith. It's all a part of the bigger picture. The universe has its own plans for you which are even better. It's shaping you to become the person who deserves the kind of life you want.

It may not be apparent right now, but it's eventually good for you.

It's very important to be positive in your present situation. Always imagine positive things happening in the future. Do not let negative thoughts stay in your head for long.

Whenever you catch yourself thinking negative thoughts, stop, take a deep breath, and imagine a positive outcome in your mind.

Find reasons to love yourself and your life. One of the best things you can do now is to align your new life with your desire. Understand that tough times have a positive effect on your journey through life.

It will lead you to what you ultimately want.

Walking on the present path may be hard initially, but have faith that it's good for you and keep moving forward.

Do not look back.

Remind yourself daily of your ultimate desire. Keeping a journal really helps too. Writing down your thoughts on paper makes you think rationally and lets you examine your life.

Now, the only thing remaining is to take massive action. As you make progress, you will start seeing how all this comes together and takes you to your ultimate desire. But till you see that silver lining, remember to have faith.

If you can see it, you can achieve it.

CHAPTER 11
FAILURE IS AN OPPORTUNITY TO LEARN

People are afraid to fail. Many people give up even before they take the first step. Thoughts like "What's the use?", "Why even try? I will never get that", "It's beyond my abilities" and "I have never achieved something like this before" race through their minds every time they go after a BIG goal.

It's very common to experience thoughts like that. All people experience fear and doubts, especially when they go after a goal which is beyond their past achievements.

But what if I tell you that you can ENSURE your success one hundred percent, and there is no such thing as a failure?

Let me introduce you to the concept of embracing change.

Contrary to what people may believe, failure is not the end of the road to success. Failure is an indicator that you need to try something different to obtain your goal. You need to change your approach, do something different if your current plan is not working, and keep trying out different approaches/plans/actions until you find something which works.

Let's suppose you are trying to get in shape. You're going to the gym six times a week and following a healthy diet plan, but still not able to lose weight. Instead of getting disheartened, collect more information - consult your dietitian, read the best books on weight loss, etc.

Find out how the human body works, how we put on fat, and how the body converts fat into energy. Find out different forms of exercises like high-intensity interval training, cross-fit, etc. New information would show you several different ways to lose weight.

Pick anyone. Make changes in your diet and exercise routine and continue it for a month or two. Look for any progress. If you don't see any improvement, make changes in our diet and exercise program yet again.

Stick to it, and look for the results. Rinse and repeat until you find a diet & exercise plan which works for you.

Success is virtually GUARANTEED if you keep trying different approaches to obtain your objective. The ONLY way you cannot succeed, is when you CHOOSE to stop trying.

Success is like finding a combination of a lock. You may need to try a few different combinations, but if you persist, you'll eventually get the lock open. Persistence, when combined with changing your approach, is the recipe for guaranteed success.

Some people may ask, "But how do I find other approach options? How would I know what to try next?"

We live in an age where information is available at every moment. There are thousands of books, eBooks, YouTube videos, seminars, audio programs, blogs, newsletters, CD and DVD programs, podcasts, and other sources available to you right now. Take advantage of them. Learn.

Most successful people in the world are constant learners. They never stop learning and improving themselves. Bill Gates was a college dropout who became one of the richest people in the world. He attributes the majority of his success to being a constant learner.

Research repeatedly shows that learning and constantly improving yourself are much more powerful predictors of success than a college degree. While it's great to have a college degree, you need to become a student for life.

When you learn, you grow. When you think you've made it and stop learning, you start going downhill.

Anthony Robbins said, "In this world, nothing is constant. Either you are growing or dying." Always keep educating yourself. You can find people who have accomplished a lot but are still learning new things every day.

Whatever your challenges, if you look for a solution, you will find it. Look around, it blows my mind that we can get millions of dollars' worth of information in a $10 soft-cover book!

Incredibly successful people, who have spent their lifetime overcoming challenges, wrote all their knowledge and experience in a little book... and you have access to it! You are fortunate enough to learn what they learned in about a fraction of the time it took them to discover all these solutions.

We are blessed to live in times like this. Think about it. You have a massive advantage over previous generations which didn't have the kinds of resources available to you now.

Learn and use this knowledge. You would discover several options to reach your destination. Pick anyone, and start taking action. Look for progress and make changes if required.

Each individual who became successful had to embrace change. Whether they had to change their attitude, behavior, plans, action, team, or something similar, it's the "change" that ultimately brought them success.

I attribute 90% of my success to persistence and embracing change. Success never came easy for me. I always had to work harder than most people to achieve my goals.

At first, I used to get frustrated about it. "Why do I always have to work this much?" I would often ask myself, "Other people seem to get by with much less effort."

But my struggles turned out to be a blessing in disguise. It forced me to analyze what I was doing wrong and learn the fundamentals of success. I spent many years studying success and created a blueprint that can be applied to become successful in ANY endeavor.

Later, I realized that I can use this knowledge to help other people overcome their challenges as well. It led to the creation of my blog and this book.

According to the evolution theory presented by Charles Darwin, species that are unable to adapt to constant change are likely to be weeded out of existence. This adaptation – change – is even more important now because our society is changing and evolving at a rapid pace.

In this day & age, businesses, as well as individuals, have to change constantly to keep up with the pace of modern evolution. Those who fail, become "extinct". Successful businesses go down, people lose their wealth, top athletes get kicked out of the competition - all because they failed to change.

On the other hand, people and businesses who DO adapt themselves to the current situation become leaders of their chosen fields. Think about the most successful individuals and corporations. Can you count how many times they had to change in order to make progress?

The popular wisdom of 'don't quit' may not enough anymore. Even if you keep going, you're still in danger of doing the same thing over and over again. It's like beating a dead horse.

You must combine 'don't quit' ideology with 'embracing change' to become wildly successful in your life.

In the past, I too fell in the trap of doing things which didn't work again & again and expecting a different result. As if a magic fairy would appear and say, "Oh you poor soul; you've worked hard enough. Let me give you what you want."

In life, success will never come from doing the WRONG things, no matter how persistent or hard-working you are.

But when you combine persistence with the willingness to change... boom!

You will succeed.

Every time.

Failure As Feedback

Whenever you achieve any result, it is feedback – either negative or positive. Positive feedback indicates, "you are going in the right direction. Keep going."

Negative feedback – failure or setback – represents, "Stop. Something is not right. It needs correction."

Always remember, when you experience failure, there is nothing to be ashamed of. You did your best at the time. Let it go and move forward. It may not feel good, but failure plays an important part in achieving success. Successful people are willing to fail more than other people in order to succeed.

"I have missed more than 9,000 shots in my career. I have lost almost 300 games. 26 times, I have been trusted to take the game-winning shot and missed. I have failed over and over again in my life. And that is why I succeed." – **Michael Jordan, basketball legend**

Any feedback, whether it FEELS good or not, contains very valuable information. It indicates if you are on the right course or not. It also highlights the need to make necessary adjustments in your plans & activities required to move forward.

Think of negative feedback (a.k.a. failure) as a clue. Instead of quitting, look at what isn't working and change it. Embrace change to such an extent that you are CONSTANTLY SEEKING feedback.

Once you start collecting feedback quickly and make the necessary corrections, you'll progress at a rapid pace. All the underlying issues will surface quickly and be dealt with. This constant refinement will make your process much smoother and efficient. Soon, you will be cruising towards success.

"Failing forward is the ability to get back up after you have been knocked down, learn from your mistake, and move forward in a better direction." – **John C. Maxwell, success coach**

Now, instead of being afraid of failure, think of it as feedback and a necessary component of success. Every successful person had to go through challenges and failures, but they looked at it as an opportunity. You must too.

Remove the whole concept of failure from your mind. There is no such thing as failure. There is only feedback.

The ONLY way you cannot succeed... is when you stop trying.

Keep moving and you will reach your destination... every time.

It's a very liberating feeling. How would you feel when you know you cannot fail, EVER? What would you achieve? What kind of goals would you go for?

Success Story of Soichiro Honda

In 1930, when Japan was taken away by the Great Depression, Soichiro Honda was still in school. In 1937, he started developing 'piston rings' in a small workshop.

He wanted to sell the idea to Toyota and worked extremely hard for it. After working day and night, Honda was finally able to complete his piston rings and took a working sample to Toyota for examination.

Toyota rejected his piston rings. Reason: it did not meet their quality standards!

He went back to school where other engineers made fun of him, but he didn't give up. For two more years, Honda worked relentlessly on the design and refinement of his piston rings.

He submitted them again to Toyota and this time won a contract!

Now, he needed a factory to supply materials to Toyota. Unfortunately, Japan was gearing for war at the time, and resources were in short supply. He couldn't find enough cement to build his factory, so he developed a new process to create cement himself!

Soon the factory was constructed and was ready to begin production. But fate had other ideas. His factory was bombed twice, and steel became unavailable at the same time.

It really tested the resolve of Soichiro Honda. But he still didn't quit, only changed his approach.

He collected gasoline cans discarded by US fighters and started using them as new raw materials in his newly rebuilt manufacturing process.

As things started to look better, an earthquake leveled his factory yet again. Any ordinary person would have given up at that point. But he persisted.

After the war, there was a huge shortage of gasoline in Japan. People began to either walk or ride their bicycles to their destination. Honda saw an opportunity and attached a tiny engine to his bicycle.

His neighbors saw it and requested one for themselves. Honda tried to meet the demands, but he couldn't, as resources like material and money were lacking.

Instead of being disappointed, he looked for possible solutions.

He wrote an inspiring letter to 18,000 bicycle shop owners to help him revitalize Japan by innovation. Out of which 5,000 responded and forwarded whatever resources they could to him.

Then he began developing small bicycle engines. Initial ones were bulky and didn't work. After continuous refinement and development, however, he created a small engine "the super club" which became quite successful.

Soon, he began exporting his bicycle engines to Europe and America, establishing the brand of Honda overseas.

Later, when the world was moving towards small cars, Honda saw an opportunity and started manufacturing small cars. His expertise in creating small engines paid dividends and Honda cars became a runaway success.

Today, the Honda Corporation has more than 175,000 employees on multiple continents and became one of the largest automobile companies in the world.

All because of Soichiro Honda's willingness to learn, take action, adapt, and a firm commitment to his dream...

CHAPTER 12
COMPARISON IS THE THIEF OF JOY

One thing important thing to remember when you are doing this is to not look at other people. Walk on your path.

You will see people who achieved success easily and begin to doubt yourself. Don't do that. Everyone is on their journey in life. The human tendency is to look at other people and compare them with ourselves. "Am I doing better than Sam? Am I doing worse than Suzy?"

It's one of the most common mistakes we make and something which you must avoid completely.

These comparisons distract you. When you make the performance of others your benchmark, you will never reach your own personal best. The only way to uncover your true potential is to focus on improving yourself and your own performance as much as possible.

The only benchmark you have to beat is your current personal best. That's it.

Trust in your own value

Don't let any compliments boost your ego, or any criticisms shake your confidence. Do your personal best at the moment and look for ways to improve it next time.

Always have complete faith in the value you are offering to the world. Your personality, thoughts, ideas are unique and that makes them special. Nobody has the same life experience and thought process as you. People will benefit from your perspective. Believe in yourself.

If you don't, how do others trust you? People look at you and see how certain you are. If you come across confident about your offer, they will try to look at it through your perspective.

A firm belief in yourself is the BASE of your ability to influence people. The more conviction you have, the more chances of people believing in you and supporting your cause.

It will increase the chance of success (financial, social, or emotional) tremendously.

Be optimistic

In life, nothing is certain. We are living in a world full of uncertainty. Whether that's good or bad, depends on how we look at it.

People fear the unknown when they expect the worst. Don't do it. Instead, make it better by thinking of uncertainty as 'freedom'. The fact that our future is not fixed in stone is liberating. We are given a choice, to create our future as we like.

Can you imagine how it would be if the future was certain and we could not do anything to change it? We are blessed to have a choice. Many people don't realize this gift and take shelter under fear.

Be optimistic and always remember - In life you get what you expect. So expect good things to happen. Find the good in people and situations.

Broadly speaking from my own experience, optimistic people generally become successful in life, and whiners & complainers end up at the bottom.

Think about people who are very successful in life and you will find that they're all optimistic. Without optimism, you would not think bigger, take a lot of action, and give value to society. It also takes a great amount of optimism to face difficult challenges on your path to success.

"Whiners & complainers will focus on the dark mountain ahead, while optimistic people tend to see the shimmer of light behind the mountain."

How to create luck?

I believe effort combined with positive expectation creates 'luck'. When you see a better future and give it all you have, you will stumble upon opportunities not visible earlier.

Then everyone starts calling you 'lucky'.

I don't believe in luck, but I have seen many instances where circumstances aligned themselves according to our 'expectations' of the future.

Optimism is a learnable skill. It can be developed with practice. Start small and expect little events in your day to be positive. For example, when you get up in the morning, say "thank you for this wonderful life". When taking shower, think "it's going to be a great day". When you are driving your car in the morning, pay attention to the natural environment around you. Listen to your favorite song and say "This is AWESOME! I LOVE THIS SONG!"

Small things like these will develop your ability to be more optimistic and focus on the good side of life. It's such a necessary component of success that I dedicated an entire chapter on cultivating a positive attitude earlier.

CHAPTER 13

CREATING POSITIVE ENERGY IN RELATIONSHIPS

Listen deeply

To create a positive, fulfilling relationship, you need to first understand others and their needs. The best way to do it is to listen deeply to what they are saying.

It's sad that in today's hectic world, where everyone is short on time, we have lost touch with our ability to truly listen. We want everything to be as short & fast as possible. Nobody has time to stop and listen.

People forget that listening to the other person is still the fastest way to win friends and make contacts. Listening does several important things: It makes the other person feel respected and we're able to understand them better.

In our 'attention-deficit' society, we all crave someone who listens to us. It makes us feel valued and respected. Let's take an example- who is your best friend?

It's likely that your best friend is someone who listens to you, doesn't interrupt, and laughs at your jokes. We are very attracted to people who listen to us. Good listeners have an infinite supply of friends. People like spending time with them and end up introducing them to their friends.

It's one of the fastest ways to expand your social network. And for that, you need to know how to BECOME a good listener.

How to listen effectively?

1) Make frequent eye contact. Avoiding eye contact will make others think you are not interested in what they are saying.

2) Fully focus on the conversation. No excessive thinking or worrying. No scanning of the environment. Just put all your attention on the words being said.

3) Try to understand the real meaning or "gist" behind the words. Look at their facial expression, tone, and emotions. What is the real message they want to convey?

4) Give appropriate responses. Nod your head. Say "um-hm". Change your facial expressions. Basically, act like a good listener. People need your responses in order to continue talking. If you just stare blankly at the speaker, they would think either you are not listening or not interested in their topic.

Practice good listening in every conversation. Get good at it. This single skill will deepen your relationships with everyone.

Show your real self

Always be real. Show your true personality. Fully express your thoughts and feelings. Many people don't because it's scary. You could get hurt. It takes courage to be yourself when the whole world is watching you.

People hide their true personality. They keep quiet and say only 'socially accepted' things. This is called 'creating a shell' around ourselves. Some people never come out of their shells. They keep hiding their true self from the outside world.

And it's a shame. Life is too short to live like that.

Instead, express your true self. Let the world know who you are and what you stand for. Maybe some people will hate you, but the majority will like and respect you for it. Everyone knows it takes courage to put your real personality on the line. You are exposing yourself to possible rejections. It takes guts.

When you open up, people notice. We all live in a stifled society where people prefer to remain quiet and closed. When someone takes a stand for who they are and express their true self, it's very attractive. We find it addictive to watch. For example, look at celebrities...

Celebrities are people who can express themselves fully even when they are under the spotlight. They openly show their personality even when the world's attention is on them. They realize few people will not like them for who they are... but it still does not stop them from being themselves. This universally attractive quality eventually win them the admiration of millions of people worldwide.

It takes courage and practice, but in the end, well worth it. Your experience of life would be much richer and satisfying. You will come across as a genuine, confident individual who inspires people to break out of their own shells.

Be assertive: Speak your mind

As an individual, you have the right to fully express your thoughts, feelings, needs & wants to others. It's called being assertive.

Many people shy away from expressing their real desires. This leads to a lot of friction in their relationships. If we don't speak up and clearly state our intentions, we will never be understood by others.

Have you ever heard someone say - "Nobody understands me" or "Nobody cares about me"? All such problems stem from not willing to assert yourself. People do not have psychic powers. They cannot read your mind. Even people who have been with you for a long time need you to express yourself... because your thoughts, needs & wants change over time.

These changes may not be apparent to you, but others can clearly see them. This creates misunderstanding, conflict, separation, divorce, and every other friction in relationships known to man.

Speak your mind. Start expressing yourself. Let people know who you are and what you need. That's the only way they can clearly understand you. It may seem like common sense, but in reality, very few people are able to assert themselves.

People are afraid of being rejected, disliked. They think if they express their desire, people would think they are greedy and selfish.

In reality, it's the other way around.

Being assertive and expressing yourself will smoothen your relationships. It will make people understand you better, and also inspire them to express THEIR needs as well. Things will be clear and every person will get a better chance to be understood. It's win-win for all involved.

Speaking of win-win...

Think Win-Win

Whenever you are dealing with people, try to meet the needs of everyone involved. Final outcomes don't need to favor any one particular party. Try to make the result beneficial for each side.

For example- your boss wants you to work overtime to finish the project early but you have other commitments. On the surface, both of your interests appear to be clashing with each other, but it's possible to turn it into a WIN-WIN situation.

One of the many possible solutions could be: you agree with your boss to work on weekends as it will let you fulfill your commitments during the week and finish the project on time as well.

Try your best to make situations win-win for all. If your intent is positive, it will come across and people will respect you for it.

Make it a habit. Look for ways to create a win-win situation every time you can. The most admired leaders have this quality. They have an image of 'solution-finders' and gained the trust of millions of people.

This is such a rare & desirable quality that if you can create a reputation for creating win-win situations, people will try to put you in leadership roles. We all want someone in authority who can produce outcomes favorable for all concerned parties.

It makes everybody feel safe under your leadership. They would realize that they are under a capable authority which will never compromise their situation.

It's a great habit that will gain you lots of friends and followers. Another benefit of making a win-win situation is the amazing satisfaction you get afterward. Nobody is left wanting. No conflicts. You have added value to each side by fulfilling their needs. You are truly making the world a better place for everyone.

Final Thoughts

You have just learned several powerful concepts and exercises to build an unshakable, rock-solid sense of positivity. These are some of my most cherished pieces of information on building an optimistic personality. I have extensively used these to change my thought process from negative to a positive one.

Now it's up to you to take this knowledge and use it wisely. Remember: without its application, knowledge has no value. But when acted upon, it has the power to change destiny.

Use this information well, and it will continue to serve you forever.

I wish you all the happiness, love, and success that you truly deserve.

All the best.

Vishal Pandey
Yourselfactualization@gmail.com

If you have enjoyed this book, please take a moment of your time to put a review on the website from where you have purchased this book. Your review will be very valuable in getting this book to reach more people who need this information.

Thank you.

About The Author

After completing post-graduation in business management, Vishal Pandey joined the corporate world, only to realize quickly that it was not the path for him. His decade-old passion for self-development led him to the world of writing and creation of his blog.

Over the course of sixteen years, he read hundreds of books, listened to audio/video programs, attended seminars on the topic of personal development, and tested every piece of information by applying it in real life.

His blog was originally created to share this information with the world but later evolved into a platform for mutual interaction with his readers. After receiving several requests to write a book from his readers, he wrote 'Success Code', followed by 'Positive Thinking' and 'Social Success'.

Besides writing, he loves meditation, yoga, martial arts, music, nutrition, psychology, human behavior, and traveling.

You can contact him at:

Email: yourselfactualization@gmail.com

Facebook: facebook.com/selfactualization.co

Twitter: @selfactualized9

More Books by Vishal Pandey

Gratitude: Getting In Touch With What Really Matters

Forgiveness: The Greatest Cure for a Suffering Heart

Winner's Mindset

Praise For The Author's Work

"Inspiring and encouraging! 5 Stars" - Reader's Favourite
(Success Code)

"An amazing work. 5 Stars!" - Candoar, Consultant, USA
(Success Code)

"Extremly motivating and uplifting book! 5 Stars" - Preeti, India
(Success Code)

"One of the best self help books I have ever read! 5 Stars!" -
Amazon customer, USA (Success Code)

"I love this book, everything you need to be better person when
dealing with other people, specially when doing business." -
Amazon customer, Mexico (Social Success)

"Extremely motivational and inspirational. 5 Stars!" - Naveen
KS, UK (Social Success)

"Great book for developing a successful social persona and
influence. 5 Stars!" - Rahul, Canada (Social Success)

"A guide to confident body language and communication. 5
Stars!" - Amazon customer, India (Social Success)

"A brilliant book on building self confidence. Helped me a lot whenever life took a dive." - Tarun, India

"I couldn't believe he had never written a book before....this one is better than 90% of all that I have read. Would highly recommend it." Linda, USA

"I strongly recommend this book. He has tackled various issues in an uncomplicated manner. An absolute must read which doesn't drag too much.5 Stars" - Amazon customer, USA

"Author gave clear guidelines on how to make changes in your mindset to ultimately make the positive changes in your life. Don't just read it and forget it. Start a journal and begin to see life in a positive light. 5 Stars!" - Amazon customer, USA

Printed in Great Britain
by Amazon